Head *to* Heart

GILA MANOLSON

WHAT TO KNOW
BEFORE
DATING AND
MARRIAGE

TARGUM/FELDHEIM

ISBN: 1-56871-997-3

Copyright © 2002, 2004 by
Gila Manolson

All rights reserved.
No part of this publication may be translated, reproduced,
stored in a retrieval system or transmitted, in any form
or by any means, electronic, mechanical, photocopying,
recording or otherwise, without prior permission
in writing from the publishers.

published by:
TARGUM PRESS, INC.
22700 W. Eleven Mile Rd.
Southfield, MI 48034
Email: targum@netvision.net.il
Fax toll free: 888-298-9992
www.targum.com

distributed by:
FELDHEIM PUBLISHERS
POB 43163 / Jerusalem, Israel
208 Airport Executive Park
Nanuet, NY 10954
www.feldheim.com

Printed in Israel

To my husband,

Avraham,

*for making our marriage
the blessing it is.*

בס"ד

Aish HaTorah
AT THE WESTERN WALL

FOUNDER AND PRESIDENT
Rabbi Noah Weinberg

WORLD CENTER
Jerusalem, Israel

BRANCHES
Boston, MA
Birmingham, AL
Cleveland, OH
Detroit, MI
Johannesburg, S. A.
Kiev, Ukraine
Los Angeles, CA
London, UK
Melbourne, Australia
Miami, FL
Minsk, Belarussia
Moscow, Russia
New York, NY
Philadelphia, PA
Santiago, Chile
St. Louis, MO
St. Petersburg, Russia
Toronto, Canada
Washington, D.C.

JERUSALEM FUND
Miami, FL
Toronto, Canada
Manhattan, NY

DISCOVERY
Jerusalem, Israel
Brooklyn, NY

JERUSALEM FELLOWSHIPS
Jerusalem, Israel
Manhattan, NY

"A stranger was I in a strange land"—So many of today's observant young adults are in that very situation, involved in the world of shidduchim without a clue as to what marriage is all about. Far worse are those who think they know what they're getting themselves into. Frum society is no longer the cozy, idealistic little community it once was. Baruch Hashem, we've grown into a vast, diverse population, but people often know little about one another or what marriage requires. It can no longer be taken for granted that husband and wife agree on their respective roles, understand that marriage is a commitment, and will do whatever it takes to make their relationship work. Nor can it even be taken for granted that a failed marriage will be terminated in a respectable manner.

Contrary to what many wish to believe, this situation prevails in all segments of our society. Having assisted couples from backgrounds that range from secular to modern to "yeshivish" and "Chassidish," my colleagues and I have encountered the problem throughout the Orthodox world.

As a seasoned lecturer on relationships in Judaism, Gila Manolson is well aware of the trouble they're in. *Head to Heart: What to Know Before Dating and Marriage* expresses the passion for truth and piercing insight she is famous for, presented in her clear, candid style. The work also reflects hours of research and consultation with Torah authorities as well as professionals to insure accuracy and fidelity to Torah values.

Head to Heart is required reading for every Orthodox person considering marriage.

May Hashem bless every Jewish home with harmony and joy, and may we merit the title "a kingdom of priests and a holy nation."

Sincerely,

Yitzchak Berkowitz

Yitzchak Berkowitz

ONE WESTERN WALL PLAZA רחבת הכותל 1, הרובע היהודי
POB 14149, Old City, Jerusalem, Israel ת.ד. 14149,(כתובת משרדים) שבות 1, העיר העתיקה, ירושלים
Tel. (972-2) 628-5666 • Fax: (972-2) 627-3172 • email: Jerusalem@Aish.edu • http://www.aish.edu

RABBI ZEV LEFF

Rabbi of Moshav Matityahu
Rosh Hayeshiva Yeshiva Gedola Matisyahu

הרב זאב לף

מרא דאתרא מושב מתתיהו
ראש הישיבה ישיבה גדולה מתתיהו

d.n. modiin   71917   ד.נ. מודיעין   tel.   08-976-1138   טל'   fax   08-976-5326   פקס

בס"ד

Head to Heart: What to Know Before Dating and Marriage presents a framework of dating and marriage that will greatly benefit many Jewish singles. Its solid, practical, and sensitive advice make it an excellent source and guide that will contribute greatly to a successful marital relationship.

Mrs. Manolson is a G-d-fearing wife and mother of admirable character as well as a learned, perceptive, and competent teacher and counselor.

I highly recommend *Head to Heart*, as I do Mrs. Manolson's other books.

Sincerely,

Rabbi Zev Leff

Moshav Shitufi   מושב שיתופי

d.n. modiin   71917   ד.נ. מודיעין
tel.   08-976-1016   טל'
fax   08-976-1124   פקס

NEVE · YERUSHALAYIM

נ ו ה · י ר ו ש ל י ם

בס״ד

PRESIDENT
Bernard Hochstein

DEAN
Rabbi Dr. Dovid Refson

DIRECTOR GENERAL
Avrohom Stefansky

NEVE
SCHOOL OF GENERAL
JEWISH STUDIES
Rabbi Moshe Chalkowski

MECHINA
Rabbi Eliezer Liff

SHALHEVET
Rabbi David Kass

ISRAELI DIVISION
Rabbi Chaim Metzger

FRENCH DIVISION
Rabbi Gerard Ackermann

RUSSIAN/CIS DIVISION
Rabbi Shlomo Nachat

BNOS CHAVA
Rabbi Dovid Abramov
Rabbi Nosson Geisler

MICHLELET ESTHER
Rabbi Boruch Smith
Rabbi Ari Winter

NEVE TEHILA
Rabbi Yair Kramer

ME'OHR BAIS YAAKOV
Rabbi Zecharya Greenwald

MAALOT YERUSHALAYIM
Phyllis Geisler

MAALOT ISRAEL
Chana Finkel

MORESHET INSTITUTE
Rabbi David Kass

BACHELOR'S DEGREE IN
SOCIAL WORK
Chaya Wexler

MASTER'S DEGREE IN
FAMILY COUNSELING
Dr. Yisrael Levitz

MASTER'S DEGREE IN SPEECH-
LANGUAGE PATHOLOGY
Jerry Koller

THERAPY CENTERS
Family Counseling
Speech and Language

REGISTRAR
Dr. Avraham Schwartzbaum

ASSOCIATE REGISTRAR
David Starr-Glass

ASSOCIATE DIRECTOR
Chaya Wexler

I often look back and realize the invaluable guidance my mentors have given me at critical times. Yet mentors are few and far between today, leaving us with little access to the education we need to prepare for marriage. As a result, divorce has skyrocketed, and with it tragedy of unprecedented scope.

In this light, *Head to Heart: What to Know Before Dating and Marriage* is a tremendous service. Gila Manolson articulates time-tested wisdom regarding relationships and offers contemporary insights into this complex and challenging area of life. A highly readable and informative work, *Head to Heart* will leave an indelible impression on thousands of lives.

Sincerely,

Tziporah Heller

Tziporah Heller

P. O. Box 43016, Beit Yitzchak Street, Har Nof, Jerusalem, Israel. Tel. (02) 654-4555. Fax (02) 651-9376
25 Broadway, New York, NY 10004. Tel. (212) 422-1110. Fax (212) 785-0898
ת.ד. 43016 רח' בית יצחק, הר נוף, ירושלים, ישראל. טלפון 654-4555 (02). פקס 651-9376 (02)

CONTENTS

Preface   9
Acknowledgments   11
Introduction   15

Part I: Setting the Stage   17

1. RE-APPROACHING DATING   19
   Challenging the Experience Principle   20
   Staying Intact   27
   Dating for Real   31

Part II: Being Ready   35

2. GROWING YOURSELF   37
   Working on the Inside   38
   The Foundation of Closeness   44
   Know Yourself   52

3. BEHIND THE "CLICK"   57
   Being Human   58
   The Unconscious Connection   60
   Wake-Up Time   64
   Becoming Aware   67

Part III: Being Wise   71

4. LOVE AND MARRIAGE   73
   The Gift of Love   73
   The Road to Oneness   80

5. AFFIRMING WOMANHOOD   89
   Tradition   91
   Change   101
   Bringing It Home   107

Part IV: Being Practical   *111*

6. LEADING WITH YOUR HEAD   113
     "We Can Work It Out"?   114
     Intelligent Dating   117
     Doing It Right   121
     A Match Made in Heaven   134

7. STEERING CLEAR OF ABUSE   137
     Red Lights   138
     Checking Yourself   153

Part V: Being Informed   *157*

8. DOLLARS AND SENSE   159
     Making "50-50" a Reality   160
     From Parent to Child   161

9. AN OUNCE OF PREVENTION   163
     Ideal and Reality   164
     Restoring Protection   167

A FINAL WORD   173

Preface

People often ask me, "What drives you to write?" The answer is simple: frustration. When I have something to say that might help people get more out of life, I become frustrated that I can't tell everyone, so I write a book.

Head to Heart offers practical and philosophical advice about preparing for dating and marriage. It is not a comprehensive guide. Other excellent books on this topic already exist, and I urge you to read them. (Check your local Jewish bookstore, or ask someone you respect for recommendations.) The purpose of this book is to add to the discussion by filling in some important missing pieces.

Head to Heart is similar in significant ways to my previous books. Like *The Magic Touch* and *Outside/Inside*, it is intended to speak to you whether you were raised in an observant home, are newly religious, or are exploring Judaism for the first time—and in addressing a very real part of life, it takes a down-to-earth, common-sense approach. While some of what I'll be saying is specifically Jewish, a great deal of it— such as practical wisdom and accepted principles in psychology—is not. At the same time, all the material presented is consonant with Torah philosophy.

This book also differs from my others. First, while *The Magic Touch* and *Outside/Inside* each had a single theme (refraining from physical relationships before marriage, and defining yourself by who you are inside), *Head to Heart* addresses a variety of interrelated topics. Part I examines the purpose of dating; Part II focuses on personal growth; Part III presents

insights into love, marriage, and Jewish womanhood;
Part IV discusses practical matters of dating; and Part
V raises halachic (Jewish legal) issues relevant to married life. While some chapters may speak to you more
than others, I believe they're all essential. Second, in
addition to ideas, I'll be presenting hard facts culled
from counselors, rabbis, hotline workers, educators,
matchmakers, therapists, and those who work in rabbinical courts. Chapters with halachic content were
also reviewed by two *poskim* (Jewish legal authorities),
whose letters of approbation appear at the beginning
of this book.

My purpose, however, is the same it's always been:
to give you more Jewish wisdom for living. No matter
who you are or what your background, I hope this
book will help you enter a rewarding, lifelong relationship, by telling you what to know before dating
and marriage.

G. M.

Jerusalem

Acknowledgments

Hashem has once again blessed me with the opportunity to write a book, and I'm indebted to all the outstanding individuals who helped it come to fruition:

First and foremost, Rabbi Yitzchak Berkowitz, *shlita*, whose sensitive and wise halachic and hashkafic guidance inspired this project;

Rabbi Zev Leff, *shlita*, for his ongoing moral and practical support;

Batya Friedman, a devoted friend and brilliant critic, without whose constant support, encouragement, depth and fine-tuned perception I can't imagine writing a book;

Debra Kershner, M.A., a highly caring professional and person, for her wise insights and generous assistance;

Marina Goodman (author of *Why Should I Stand behind the Mechitzah When I Could Be a Prayer Leader? The Traditional Response for the Contemporary Woman*), an unexpected gold mine of astute observations and on-the-mark suggestions;

Rebbetzin Tziporah Heller, author of *More Precious than Pearls: Selected Insights into the Qualities of the Ideal Woman*, for so much of what I appreciate about Jewish womanhood, and for her perceptive review of the manuscript;

Another exceptional teacher, for what I understand about why women are changing;

All the others who graciously contributed their expertise, including Miriam Adahan, Ph.D. and author of *Living with Difficult People (Including*

Yourself); Jeff Auerbach, Psy.D. and author of *How to Irritate the Ones You Love: A Concise, Practical Guide to the True Nature of Relationships*; Rabbi Michael Broyde, dayan in the Beit Din of America and law professor at Emory University; matchmaker Heather Cirota; Rosie Einhorn, L.C.S.W. and coauthor of *Talking Tachlis: A Singles' Strategy for Marriage*; Rebbetzin Lea Feldman; Lynn Finson, M.S.; Rachel Frumin, M.S.; Debby Gross, director of the Crisis Center for Religious Women in Jerusalem; Rachel Levmore, rabbinical court advocate; Shaya Ostrov, C.S.W. and author of *The Inner Circle: Seven Gates to Marriage*; Miriam Reinfeld, Ph.D.; Sarah Schneider, author of *Kabbalistic Writings on the Nature of Masculine and Feminine* (available at www.amyis rael.co.il/smallvoice); Phyllis Strauss, Ph.D.; Deborah Tobin, Ph.D.; and two women from the Educational Prevention Program of the Shalom Task Force in New York;

Two wonderful educators for whose input I am grateful: Rabbi Dr. Natan T. Lopes Cardozo; and Dr. Michael Kaufman, author of *Love, Marriage, and Family in Jewish Law and Tradition*;

All the other special individuals who offered help and/or feedback, including Shaina Buchwald, Miriam Ciner, Israel Ellen, Elana Epstein (our incomparable *bat bayit*), Dena Estrin, Leat Galimidi, Marina Gelfand, Chana Levitan, Tova Saul, Leah Schachter, David Teten, and Moshe Zeldman; and with particular thanks to Tamar Bezalely, Stuart Green, Leon Aaron Kenin, and Brett Weil;

The many authors (in addition to those cited in the text) whose books have influenced my thinking, including Reuven P. Bulka, author of *Jewish Marriage:*

A Halakhic Ethic; Aharon Feldman, author of *The River, the Kettle and the Bird: A Torah Guide to Successful Marriage*; Manis Friedman, author of *Doesn't Anyone Blush Anymore? Reclaiming Intimacy, Modesty and Sexuality*; Lawrence Kelemen, author of *To Kindle a Soul: Ancient Wisdom for Modern Parents and Teachers*; Maurice Lamm, author of *The Jewish Way in Love and Marriage*; and Wendy Shalit, author of *A Return to Modesty: Discovering the Lost Virtue* (from whose review my manuscript also benefited);

My loving and deeply beloved children, Chananya, Elyashiv, Yair, Temima, Emuna, Ayelet, and Yisrael, for good-naturedly tolerating the time I've dedicated to writing;

And finally, Avraham, my soulmate, for everything.

Introduction

Marriage always entails surprises. Some may be delightful; others less so. This book was written to help you experience more delight and fewer rude awakenings. More directly, it's intended to help you get into a marriage with the best chance of meeting your hopes and expectations, bringing you the most happiness possible.

Living in the early 21st century, you have a lot to contend with. Increasingly, relationships aren't working out the way they should. Many people "fall in love" and marry with no real idea of what love and marriage are. Others are led heart-first into difficult relationships, sometimes with abusive partners, by forces they're not even conscious of. In the end, more couples divorce than stay together. When I encountered Judaism and became observant at age 22, I felt I'd been rescued from a sea of craziness and set down on an island of sanity. In time, however, I realized that the problems plaguing society at large also affect the Jewish world, which is grappling with its own issues, such as difficulties in the divorce process and the question of feminism.

Fortunately, you can avoid most of these troubles if you approach dating and marriage as you would any other major undertaking. You don't get into a top university, score high on your graduate-school entrance exams, or ace a job interview without investing considerable time and effort. Dating and marriage—success in which will contribute more to your happiness than nearly anything else—also require preparation. The time to start is not three months before the wedding (or after), but *now*. Singlehood is not a way-station to be passed through as mindlessly as possible on the road to couplehood. It is meant to be *used*, and used intelligently—for thinking, learning, and most of all growing. If you choose to acquire the wisdom and do the work, you can experience a deeply rewarding, lifelong relationship.

This book will help you get there.

Note: All the stories I'll be sharing are either true or based on real people and incidents. Names have been changed.

Part I
Setting the Stage

"Going out" means different things to different people. Chapter 1, "Re-approaching Dating," tackles the issue that precedes all others: the purpose of dating.

Chapter One
Re-approaching Dating

Dating is the emotional hub of most unmarried people's lives. If you're seeing someone (or hope to be), you may still think about school or work, but you're probably thinking more about your next date. I want you to look at dating from a new angle, and as honestly as you can, because I want to question some of the conventional wisdom surrounding it.

People date for many reasons. When I ask teenagers or other not yet marriage-minded singles why they go out, they usually answer:

"Fun."

"Attraction."

"Hormones."

"Everyone's doing it."

"So you don't have to be alone."

When I ask them why they think *others* date, they suggest:

"Social status."

"Security."

"Ego."

And when I ask more sensitive individuals why they date, they respond: "To have someone to share with and feel close to."

I could say a lot about these answers, but in my opinion, none of them is a good reason for dating. When you date, you allow someone to develop strong feelings for you, and that isn't fair to the other person if you're primarily interested in something other than a sincere relationship. And while dating may make you feel warm and wanted, it won't cure you of loneliness or insecurity in the long run. Nor will it satisfy your longing (conscious or unconscious) for genuine, soul-to-soul closeness.

Yet there's a more compelling argument for dating: "Dating many people enhances your personal development. It teaches you relationship skills, helps you understand the opposite sex, and reveals your needs. It's the most effective way to learn how to choose the right person and make marriage work." In other words, dating prepares you for the real thing. Parents who subscribe to this idea often dissuade their teens from long-term relationships for fear of stunting their emotional growth, and worry if their kids marry their first boyfriend or girlfriend. Without a lot of dating experience, how could they possibly be ready?

Dating, then, is Preparation for Marriage. Of all the reasons for becoming involved in relationships, this one sounds the most intelligent. But is it?

Challenging the Experience Principle

Does more dating experience lead to better marriages?

Let's look at our world. Most people are chalking up an impressive amount of relationship experience, starting younger and younger and involving numerous partners and considerable physical contact. Accordingly, we should be extremely wise, personally developed, and basking in marital bliss. Yet according to a 1995 report of the Council on Families in

America,* the probability of a newlywed couple ending up divorced or permanently separated was a stag-
gering 60%. Add those who stay together despite their
unhappiness, and modern marriage emerges an overwhelming failure. All this dating experience is appar-
ently not paying off.

Some argue, of course, that marriage has always
been bankrupt. While serving a societal purpose, perhaps it simply cannot deliver lasting love and happiness, and is disintegrating now only because divorce
has become more acceptable (and for women, economically feasible). "Don't even think about forever,"
I've heard people say. "Take a relationship for whatever it is, and move on when it's over." In other
words, we should stop fantasizing and be realistic.

Yet we Jews believe in marriage. We know that
with enough work, two people can enjoy a deeply satisfying, lifelong love. We also suspect that, in their
heart of hearts, even the most disillusioned cynics
haven't despaired of such a relationship. But we don't
believe experience is the way to get there.

So how did "experiential dating" become so popular?

From the beginning of modern history until the
middle of the last century, the practical aspects of marriage underwent no major upheavals from generation
to generation. Social and sexual mores, gender roles,
and marital expectations shifted only gradually, if at
all. But then came the '60s. Overnight, young adults

---

*"Marriage in America: A Report to the Nation, 1995," available from
the Institute for American Values, 1841 Broadway, Suite 211, New
York, NY 10023.

redefined masculinity, femininity, and relationships, put marriage on hold, and celebrated their new sexual freedom. In ten short years, the status quo was blown apart. When my friends and I came of age, society was still shaking from the aftershocks—and people felt that *everything* about men and women had changed, including love. Our parents had plenty of advice about colleges and careers, but not about relationships. The message many of us got was: "Look, we know what makes our marriage work. But the world's a different place now. So go get experience. Figure things out. And good luck to you."

So my generation went out and got Experience—with catastrophic results. And most young people today are still doing the same.

Don't get me wrong. You'll certainly learn from dating, but not necessarily how to succeed in marriage. Following a break-up, you may learn where you need to grow, or only where your ex does. You may learn why you keep attracting the wrong people, or why the opposite sex can't be trusted. You may learn how to achieve love, or that it's an impossible dream.

Some years ago, I spoke with a single professional hardened by years of failed relationships. "Experience has taught me to stop hoping," she informed me flatly. "I've learned to become so independent that I don't even care if there's a man in my life." Yet what she'd "learned" would only make her less likely to ever get the love that, beneath her pain and denial, she still longed for. Dating may be educational, but education isn't always wisdom.

At the same time, any wisdom you do gain will prove largely irrelevant once you marry. Marriage is entirely different from even the most long-term, committed relationship. (It's also totally unlike living together, which for most people is merely "playing house.") In forcing two "I"s into a non-negotiable "we," marriage requires tremendous self-transformation. Furthermore, before things are signed and sealed, you're each partly on your best behavior, even if subconsciously. Once your relationship is "for keeps," the real you comes out.

I know a couple who dated a long time before marrying. One Sunday morning shortly after their wedding, the husband announced he was going into the office.

"Since when do you work on Sundays?" his wife asked in surprise.

"I haven't till now, but I'm starting."

"But what about our Sunday brunch?"

"I know, honey, but it's time I got a promotion, and this is the way to do it."

"But you've always seemed relaxed about your job and about money."

"Well, if I'm going to get ahead, that'll have to change."

As this little episode illustrates, *unpredictable things come up in marriage.* An independent-minded single woman may, as a wife, now want lots of together time with her spouse. A doting fiancé may, as a husband, suddenly need to "do his own thing." Workaholics come out of the closet. And often, marriage exposes more traditional role expectations than may have surfaced during dating. All this means that, while an unmarried couple may know the "rules" of their relationship, *marriage is a whole new ballgame.* And here's where premarital experience can actually backfire. For while learning a new sport can be difficult, *it's doubly frustrating when you thought you already knew how to play*. The resulting disappointment and discouragement can even ruin the marriage. (It's no surprise, then, that according to studies cited by Dr. David Myers in *The Pursuit of Happiness*, couples who live together before marriage are far more likely to divorce than those who don't.)

In short, dating may teach you how to date, but won't teach you how to be married, and the illusion that it does can be harmful. Marriage should be approached with an open mind and as few preconceptions as possible. It's a new experience.

So how can you amass the wisdom and growth necessary for a successful marriage? The answer is simple. While many practical aspects of marriage (such as who's the cook and who's the breadwinner) may have changed over the years, what makes love last has not. Each generation need not reinvent the wheel through hard-earned experience. The learning opportunities we need have always been there, and still are, without having to date.

Let's briefly look at what a good marriage requires. To begin with, each partner must possess a reasonably healthy, adult personality. This asset includes maturity, autonomy, self-esteem, trust, the capacity for emotional intimacy, and self-knowledge (all of which will be discussed in Chapter 2). These traits needn't be acquired in dating—they should be acquired in *life*. Dating only distracts us from giving them attention. Questions such as "Do I look my best?" "Am I making a good impression?" "Will she want to go out again?" "Is this going where I hope it will?" and "Will he want to stay with me?" don't leave much time and energy to ponder if you're developing the qualities necessary for a successful marriage. Consequently, there's no reason to believe you'll gain the maturity or self-knowledge you'll need. You're even less likely to become capable of genuine intimacy, as intimacy depends largely on trust, and breakups (an inevitable part of dating) erode it. The emotional dependency dating often fosters won't help you achieve autonomy. And self-esteem, the key to everything (including true intimacy), is more apt to suffer than thrive in transient relationships, where we're seldom appreciated for who we really are.

I recall how many of my school classmates transformed once they began going out. Despite all they had going for themselves, their popularity suddenly hinged on attracting the opposite sex. The greater their success, the greater their loss of self. And once you're hooked on approval (particularly this kind), it can be hard to wean yourself. Yet a mature, satisfying relationship demands *self*-esteem, based on who you are not on the outside but on the inside, and coming not from others but from yourself.

Partners in a good marriage must also understand what love and marriage are (to be discussed in Chapter 4). Despite the changes brought by the women's movement and the sexual revolution, love and marriage haven't become something entirely new. Their essence is eternal, which means they needn't be figured out the hard way. Judaism is the best teacher; relationships are among the worst. Dating rarely involves true love (no matter what we may think at the time) and is therefore far better at teaching us what love *isn't* than what it is. And as we've seen, a grasp of marriage is unlikely to materialize from a relationship other than marriage.

A successful marriage also requires an understanding of gender differences. People often assume they'll acquire this insight too by going out. Yet dating veterans who later married will tell you how wrong this supposition is.

Joel and Liz became religious in their mid-twenties and married a few years later. I saw Liz two months after the wedding. "I figured that having had a couple of long-term girlfriends would have taught Joel something about women," she told me frankly. "But the guy knows nothing. Several times a day I have to explain, 'Honey, I'm a woman, and women feel…,' or 'That might work for you, because you're male, but I need….' He's *clueless*."

"But, of course, you completely understand your husband?" I asked with a grin.

She smiled ruefully. "If you want to know the truth, despite my own past relationships, I'm equally in the dark about men."

If dating so enlightens us about the opposite sex, millions of adult couples wouldn't be devouring John Gray's *Men Are from Mars, Women Are from Venus*. Rather than dating, books are probably the best way to get this gender education, both before and during marriage. And get it you must, for one purpose of marriage is that you learn to live with, give to, and love someone fundamentally different from you, thereby coming to appreciate the world through another's eyes.

So if you're putting a lot of time and energy into dating, chances are you aren't getting as much out of it as you may believe. Rosie Einhorn, a popular pre-marital counselor (and coauthor of *Talking Tachlis*), puts it more bluntly: "All this experience is worthless."

Staying Intact

Even if experience cost us only time and sense, that would be sad enough. Life is short, and it's a shame to spend it figuring out the basics instead of reaping the rewards of existing knowledge. Yet experience also takes its toll emotionally.

A relationship isn't a game. It means sharing, creating an opening for intimacy, being vulnerable. So, if and when it ends, it hurts. "I feel I left part of myself with my ex-girlfriend," a young man once told me. "And once you give of yourself, you can't just take it back. Now I'm afraid to let that happen again." Even one breakup can leave you too mistrusting to invest in another relationship.

When the secular world weighs emotional intactness against experience, the latter is the sure-fire winner. Experience, after all, bestows worldliness and sophistication, supposedly your ticket into adulthood. But emotional intactness? Many people don't even know what it means. If they do, they'll assume you naturally discard it with age, like a lizard sheds its skin. If that's the price of experience—well, they'll shrug, it's all part of growing up.

Jewish tradition sees things differently. Worldliness

and sophistication may be helpful or harmful; in and of themselves, they're definitely not values (and they're by no means synonymous with wisdom). But emotional health? A heart in one piece, an ability to trust, to believe things will work out, to feel life is good? These qualities are precious—and while they depend initially upon your upbringing, later relationships can make or break them. Given the high cost of experience, there's a lot to be said for innocence. And that doesn't mean naiveté, for as I've said, there are other (and far better) ways to learn about life than trial and error.

Even if you knew a breakup would leave you no worse for the wear, you can't predict your ex-partner's reaction. Dating for experience, therefore, isn't very sensitive. It could even be using someone.

You may be startled at such harsh language. But this reality was illustrated for me by Sandra, a world traveler who'd logged many brief relationships in her globetrotting.

"I disagree with your whole argument against experience," she declared. "Without all the experiences I've had, I wouldn't be who I am today. I wouldn't know myself as well as I do, I wouldn't have the understanding of men that I have, I wouldn't have the social self-confidence that I—"

"'I, I, I,'" I cut her off. "What about all those guys? Could one of them have felt more for you than either of you intended? Could he even have felt used when you said, 'Nice knowing you. You've been a great learning experience for me'?"

Sandra was taken aback. "That's not fair," she

objected. "Every man I met agreed to a short-term relationship because he knew he'd also get something out of it. It wasn't just for me—it was for him too."

"Hmm. So you really meant to say, 'If *we* hadn't had all the experiences *we*'ve had, *we* wouldn't be who *we* are today.'"

She looked uncomfortable.

"In other words, instead of using him for your own growth, you were using each other. Is that any better?"

Now Sandra really bristled. "What's wrong with it?" she retorted. "We were consenting adults."

Unfortunately for experience-seekers, there's no concept of "consenting adults" in Judaism. That two grown-ups agree to do something together privately that won't hurt anyone else doesn't mean it's okay. They could be hurting themselves. Worse, one of them could be taking advantage of someone who doesn't know better, or who's in denial about the deeper relationship he or she really wants. "Consenting adults" is usually a sophisticated excuse for selfishness. Secular law may have no problem with that, but Jewish law cares about emotional and spiritual well-being, which includes knowing how to love. Two people out for experience and pleasure are looking to *get*. Love, in contrast, is about looking to *give*.

Of course, Sandra's example is extreme. Even if you're in the "experience mode," you may seek something more than a two-week fling in a foreign country. But there's still a problem. Whether or not we acknowledge it, every relationship feeds our unconscious hope of attaining intimacy and completion. Yet if it's not commitment-oriented, it's going to end—

and we know it.

A friend recently reassessed her premarital dating experience: "I was always a good girlfriend—nice, sweet, and caring—and never intended to cause anyone pain. But each time I realized a relationship couldn't lead anywhere and broke up with a boyfriend, he was badly hurt. His trust was damaged, and I knew he wouldn't give to someone as he'd given to me for a long time. Only in hindsight do I see that the dating system is inherently flawed."

Jenny, too, learned this the hard way. A 24-year-old tourist in Israel, she wasn't looking for a serious relationship when she met Uri, a 22-year-old sabra (native-born Israeli). In no time she found herself romantically involved, and far more than she expected. "Every moment with him is heaven," she told me blissfully. Three months later, she was crying her eyes out. After a minor argument, Uri had inexplicably broken up with her. Upon closer examination, his reason became clear. As their relationship developed, Jenny had realized how much she longed for a husband and children. Uri, however, had recently completed his army service and entered university, and he wasn't ready to settle down. Sensing that Jenny wanted more than he was prepared to give, he used their argument as an excuse to terminate the relationship—and Jenny was left with a broken heart.

Few relationships lead to commitment unless each partner initially wants it. No matter how good and kind each is, one or both will get hurt. Even when dating doesn't entail "using" someone, insensitivity is built in. We're playing with some of the deepest parts of ourselves.

So think twice before involving yourself and any-one else in a relationship unlikely to go anywhere (whether because you're not sticking around, he or she isn't what you're looking for, or you're not ready for anything serious). Everyone does it, but that doesn't make it right. Dating while you're still in the "experience" stage means disregarding both the other's feelings and your own.

Dating for Real

By now, the point should be clear. "Experience is the best teacher" is rarely true in relationships, and even when it is, it's definitely the harder and less intelligent way to learn. Plugging into pre-existent wisdom and working on yourself is far more effective, more sensitive, and less painful.

In traditional Judaism, therefore, dating isn't for experience. First you grow into someone who can make a relationship work. Then you date because you want to make a lifelong commitment to another per-son—in other words, because you're ready for mar-riage.

Let me say a few words about marriage, since just mentioning "the 'M' word" makes some people shud-der. After all, marriage is scary. It means constantly considering another's needs, desires, and feelings, and never again living only for yourself. And that is exactly its purpose. Marriage asks that we become fully adult. It challenges us to overcome our natural selfishness and make room for someone else at the center of our lives—permanently.

I knew someone who, faced with this challenge, literally turned tail and ran. At age 23, Tom left his young wife and daughter, bought a motorcycle, and took off. After traveling the world for 25 years, he landed in Israel, where he settled into a tiny cave on a beach in the Sinai desert. When I met him, in his 60s, he was still living in that cave, enjoying the occasional company of soldiers and tourists, and reveling in his freedom. While he claimed to be happy, looking at him made me terribly sad. In fleeing commitment, he had lost out on love. He was still a child—and deeply alone.

Whether your encounters are in the wilderness or on the (equally uncivilized) urban singles' scene, *avoiding commitment means not growing up.* Anyone can say, "I want to be with you," or even "I want a long-term relationship" (or an "LTR," as it appears in personal ads). But what separates the men from the boys (and the women from the girls) is the ability to say "I want to *marry* you." Marriage. And that—as opposed to experience—is what dating should be for.

I once addressed a group of young men from somewhat religious homes on this topic, and as the discussion progressed, they grew less and less happy. By the time I concluded, I beheld a silent room full of extremely glum faces. Finally, a guy in the front row hesitantly raised his hand.

"Mrs. Manolson," he said slowly, "you've said dating should be for marriage. And none of us here is ready to get married. So"—he paused, almost afraid to continue—"does that mean... are you saying... none of us should be dating?"

No point in beating around the bush. "You got it," I replied.

There was a moment's silence as the terrible truth sank in. Then, looking totally forlorn, he asked, "Well, what are we supposed to be doing?"

A second guy immediately piped up (not sounding any happier than the first), "Learning Torah, right?"

"That's right," I answered. "But 'learning Torah' means more than just working on understanding a piece of Talmud. It means working on *yourself*. So do it, because someday, a very special woman will be grateful you did—and so will you."

To find the right person, you must *be* the right person, and that comes not from dating, but from real wisdom and focused inner work. So consider reversing the popular approach to dating. *First* devote yourself to the step most people skip in their headlong rush into relationships, and become somebody who can have one that will last a lifetime. *Then* date to find the right partner with whom to have it.

Taking a break from dating may not be easy at first. But the benefits will soon become clear. For one, your same-sex friendships are bound to be enriched.

"Since I stopped dating, I've become much closer to my female friends," a young woman named Jamie told me. "Half our conversations used to revolve around guys and male-related problems—like two of us being interested in the same guy, or someone feeling like a third wheel when her best friend had a boyfriend and she didn't. Now, instead of competing and sidelining, there's bonding and sharing. We talk about important things, like what we believe in, who we are, and who we want to be. And the more I discover myself, the more I appreciate my friends."

Jamie could have added that these friendships also

help build the sense of self that allows you to feel good without a boyfriend's or girlfriend's affirmation, which in turn makes you more likely to end up with the right person for the right reasons. (More about this in the next chapter.)

But calling a time-out on dating will do even more. For the energy you once expended on the opposite sex will be freed for growth—and knowing you're growing feels really good. It may (at least in the short term) even feel better than dating. One thing is for sure: It will prepare you for marriage as nothing else will. Think about it—because the best thing you can bring to marriage is a great you.

Part II
Being Ready

You wake up one morning. The sun is shining and the world feels full of promise. You think how wonderful it would be to share your life with another person. "You know what?" you say to yourself. "I think I'm ready to get married."

What you really mean is, "I think I *want* to get married." Wanting it doesn't mean you're *ready* for it, however. Being ready for marriage means reaching a certain point—and it's not the "right age," the "right level" of religious observance, or even feeling incomplete without the "right person." It's attaining a critical amount of wisdom, growth, and self-knowledge—and that takes time and work.

So let's get started. Chapter 2, "Growing Yourself," discusses the qualities to develop in order to become a good partner. Chapter 3, "Behind the 'Click,'" illuminates the psychological forces behind attraction.

Chapter Two
Growing Yourself

A couple of my friends once wanted to do something new and exciting. So they went parachuting.

First they completed several hours of training. They listened as the instructor explained how a parachute works. They learned the proper position for the first seconds of free fall, how to steer once the chute pulled open, and how to access the safety chute if it didn't. They were taught how to absorb the shock of landing by bending their knees and rolling. After class, they went outside and practiced on the ground, over and over. Finally, they put on their gear, boarded the plane, and took off. Each executed a perfect jump. And it was exhilarating.

Getting married is far more exciting—but, like parachuting, you need a lot of preparation before "taking the leap." You have to learn what a successful marriage takes. Then you have to practice—not in dating (for reasons I explained in the previous chapter) but everywhere else, because *your marriage can be only as good as your other human relationships.* Put even more broadly, *you will be only as good a spouse as you are a person.* The first step in marriage preparation, then, is *working on yourself.*

Working on the Inside

How does one become a better person?

Western society urges us to stay young. Advertisers idealize good looks, fun, and freedom from responsibility, and the younger you are, the more of these you're likely to enjoy. People often aspire not only to a youthful appearance, but to youthful attitudes and behaviors. (I was recently told that the textbook definition of adolescence now includes adults up to age 25—and I hear that, in some states, it goes up to 40.)

Popular culture, however, has a poor track record in marriage. One reason is that a successful, lifetime relationship requires not youth but *maturity*. Society, unfortunately, assumes that even the most childish adult is mature enough to marry. As Lisa Aiken points out in *Beyond Beshert: A Guide to Dating and Marriage Enrichment*, you must pass a test to get a driver's license, but not to get a marriage license. Yet emotional maturity, like driving skills, doesn't necessarily correlate with age. I remember how shocked I was when a 17-year-old girl from a very traditional, religious home told me she was engaged—until I realized she was more mature than I'd been when I married at 26. Emotional maturity is a product of upbringing and self-development. And while you can't change the way you were raised, you *can* make yourself into the person you want to be.

No one of us is fully child or fully adult; we're all somewhere in between, hopefully always moving toward adulthood. If you've never been in a successful marriage, it can be hard to know how much maturity it takes, and whether you have it. One thing you can do is ask someone who *has* been happily married for many years, knows you well, and will answer honestly. (I did this at age 23, and the rabbi diplomatically replied, "You still have potential to realize as a single.") Getting a clearer picture of where you may need to grow, however, requires a bit more introspection. Ask yourself the following questions—or better yet, ask them of a couple of good friends, and assure them you'll still be on speaking terms if they tell you the truth:

Am I honest?
1. Am I open to seeing myself for who I am?
2. Can I accept criticism and admit when I'm wrong?

Am I self-disciplined?
3. Am I patient?
4. Can I exercise self-control?
5. Can I delay gratification?

Do I put things in perspective?
6. Can I distinguish between what's more and less important in life?
7. Can I emphasize satisfactions over frustrations?
8. Do I have a sense of humor?

Am I responsible?
9. Can I persevere in order to achieve?
10. Am I dependable?

Am I realistic?
11. Am I prepared (at least intellectually) to not get everything I want?

Do I want to grow?
12. *Am I committed to becoming a better person?*

My friend Meredith once shared her perspective on why it pays to start this work before marriage. "I've always been defensive," she told me, "and that's usually why my husband and I argue—he says something intended to be helpful, I take it as criticism and get upset, then he gets upset, and it escalates. Had I begun tackling this issue when I was single, I could have avoided the much harder and slower work now." (Over-sensitivity to criticism usually points to a self-esteem issue—see ahead.)

You may have noticed a common denominator in the 12 traits listed above: seeing beyond yourself and beyond the present. This ability distinguishes children from adults, and most of us have it to some degree. Yet we all lapse into self-centered thinking and behavior.

"These speed bumps make me crazy," a taxi driver once grumbled as we entered my neighborhood.

"Thousands of children live here," I told him politely, "and there have been several terrible accidents due to speeding."

"All I know is every two seconds I have to slow down. It's ridiculous!" he complained.

"Don't you think protecting kids is more important?" I asked him directly.

"How far do you want to take it?" he retorted. "While we're at it, we might as well go back to the horse and buggy."

That's a grown man displaying the emotional maturity of a 5-year-old. We all regress when grumpy, but we have to fight it. We must constantly strive to view the world through a wider-angle lens.

Along with expanding your perception of life, emotional maturity involves focusing on others' needs, desires, and feelings. Fortunately, God created us in such a way that caring about another feels good.

At the same time, if we give just to feel good, we're missing the boat. Many years ago, inspired by what I thought was altruism, I called a local hospital and volunteered to provide musical entertainment in the children's ward.

"That's a very nice offer," the woman I spoke to told me, "but right now we're short-handed and need more basic help, like wheeling kids around, dressing and feeding them."

I was disappointed. "But I want to sing and play guitar for the children."

The woman gave it to me straight. "Are you looking to do what *you* want, or what our children need?"

Self-absorption is prevalent in our society, to the point where even giving can be tainted by self-interest. Self-centered giving is certainly better than no giving, but it should be a stepping stone to genuine concern for others and their needs. Emotional maturity in relationships means being *other-oriented*.

So take a good look at how you relate to friends, roommates, coworkers, siblings, and yes, even parents, and ask yourself more questions (or, again, pose them to people close to you):

Am I giving?
13. Can I put another's needs and desires before, or at least on a par with, my own?
14. Can I share without "keeping score"?

Am I sensitive?
>   15. Am I attentive and receptive to others?
>   16. Do I try to be aware of others' feelings?
>   17. Can I empathize and identify?
>   18. Can I nurture, comfort, and support?

Am I respectful?
>   19. Can I tolerate differences and appreciate individuality?
>   20. Can I validate perspectives I disagree with?
>   21. Can I respect others' boundaries and privacy?

Can I communicate effectively?
>   22. Can I share positive feelings?
>   23. Can I communicate negative feelings without attacking?

Am I flexible?
>   24. Can I resolve conflicts through discussion and negotiation?
>   25. Can I concede?

Can I love others despite their flaws?
>   26. Can I connect to someone even when angry at him or her?
>   27. Can I emphasize goodness amid faults?
>   28. Am I willing to stick with a relationship through good times and bad?

As I said, all these traits entail focusing on others. Stop from time to time during your interactions and think, "How much am I thinking about *her* interests as opposed to *mine*?" "Can I step out of *my* shoes and put myself in *his*?" This simple but eye-opening exercise can propel you toward greater other-orientation.

If you answered most of the 28 questions with a fairly honest "yes," you're mature enough to launch a successful relationship. If your responses are less positive, you have some work to do first. Give yourself a huge pat on the back for looking at yourself honestly and wanting to grow. Then get started. Study what the Torah has to say about personal development. Attend classes, listen to tapes, and read books. Even better, spend time with people whose marriages you admire. Ideally, apprentice in some model couple's household. (Many families will welcome you, especially if you're the helpful sort. I don't know if my husband and I qualify as a model couple, but we can always use a hand.) Observe how the husband and wife treat their kids and each other. Etch their behaviors into your being. Most importantly, try out what you learn in your own relationships.

One of the best ways to grow is simply to help people. Marriage runs on *chesed* (acts of kindness), so start developing your "giving muscles." Volunteer regularly. Look to give in your daily life. To really stretch yourself, occasionally agree to do something you really dislike. (I've learned to say "yes" before I have time to think about it: "Sheila Green is sick and desperately needs several hours of sleep, but her toddler has diarrhea and is constantly kvetching. Do you think you could babysi—" "*Yes.*") And keep reminding yourself that a special person will love you for all your effort to become the best you possible.

As you can see, I'm talking about real work—and it's natural to resist that, especially if you're tired of being single and chafing to "get on with life." A young woman who was far from ready for marriage asked me impatiently, "Plenty of immature people get married and grow up afterward—why can't I?" You can. But do you really want to be an immature spouse to someone you love? Furthermore, you'll likely be drawn to someone no more mature than yourself (and that maturity may be lower than you think). In other words, *what you are is what you'll get*. So ask yourself: Am I prepared to marry someone like me? And am I willing to suffer more marital struggles—and possible divorce—rather than growing before marriage?

If you answered no to any of the above, overcome the urge to jump into marriage before you're ready. *Picture the kind of person you want to marry, and try to become the kind of person he or she will want.* You needn't reach perfection (or even come close), or you'd have nothing to accomplish after marrying. But you want to be able to create a relationship in which you and your partner can continue growing together, with as little pain and as much joy as possible.

The Foundation of Closeness

In addition to maturity, at least four qualities contribute to a successful marriage: *autonomy*, *self-esteem*, *trust*, and *capacity for emotional intimacy*. It's important to understand these attributes, their source, and why they're essential.

A*utonomy* means seeing yourself as a self-directed person of independent value. If you're autonomous, you know who you are, stand on your own two feet, and go where you want to go. Unfortunately, many people depend too much on others, even panicking at being alone. I had a high school friend whose parents separated. In despair, her mother committed suicide. That's an extreme lack of autonomy. Less extreme examples are far more widespread.

"But aren't you supposed to feel incomplete before you marry?" you may ask. Yes—but feeling incomplete isn't being needy and insecure. Healthy dependency means recognizing your aloneness. *Unhealthy* dependency means fearing it. For an insecure person, aloneness means having no source of validation or, in more serious cases, identity. Such a person is desperate to be with someone—anyone—and I don't have to tell you how dangerous that is. Many times I've told a young person, "Before you can have a good relationship, you must learn how to live without one." An autonomous person deeply desires to share his or her life with another, but is solid as an individual.

One way to gauge your autonomy level is to observe your attitude to others. If you're overly dependent, you'll constantly worry, "What do they think of me?" If you're more autonomous, you'll ask, "What do I think of them?"

Self-esteem underlies many of the above-listed elements of emotional maturity and is the single most important ingredient in a successful relationship. Self-esteem is not a pop-psychology buzzword for "feeling good about yourself." It's built on *being* good, competent, and lovable, and recognizing it. Being a good person requires working on your character; being competent necessitates developing your abilities; and if you're a decent human being, you're already inherently lovable in God's eyes (the only One whose opinion really counts).

How lovable you feel, however, may depend on your upbringing. I know a man named Daryl who was shown love only when "performing" academically or athletically, so he can't believe he's lovable unless he excels. Robert's parents, on the other hand, accepted him unconditionally, so he nearly always feels good about himself. If you question your entitlement to love, your childhood may help you understand how your self-image developed and affected you, and how to paint a more reality-based, lovable "self-portrait."

Self-esteem must also combat advertisements, television, and movies, which substitute artificial values (such as looks, money, and glamour) for the cornerstones of genuine self-worth. Men's and women's magazines are the worst. Their very purpose is to make you feel inadequate (unless you buy their sponsors' products). For a healthy, deeply rooted sense of self, *ignore the media*. And avoid comparisons, whether to magazine models or to your next-door neighbors, unless they inspire personal growth. Self-esteem rests not on measuring up to others, but on looking at *yourself* and liking what you see.

You can probably guess why self-esteem is fundamental to a successful relationship. It lets you know the love you give is meaningful, and the love you receive is deserved. A newly married woman came to me with a classic self-esteem problem. "When my husband tells me he loves me, I can't completely accept it," she confessed. "Part of me thinks, 'Boy, I must have really fooled him about who I am.' I feel like an impostor." After acknowledging her overly critical upbringing, she was able to develop the self-worth to fully receive her husband's love.

Self-esteem also figures prominently in your unconscious choice of a marriage partner and in the success of your marital relationship. Like attracts like, so you'll most likely find yourself with someone whose self-image is as strong or weak (outwardly or inwardly) as yours. If your self-esteem is high, chances are your partner's will be as well, and you'll interact positively. For self-esteem eliminates competition, allowing you to nurture another. It brings down the walls of defensiveness, enabling you and your partner to achieve genuine understanding. It lets you accept criticism without being shattered, because you're open-minded and willing to change.

Someone I know once demonstrated this truth. One day, as I knocked on the Cohens' apartment door, another neighbor opened hers. "Are you looking for Mrs. Cohen?" she inquired.

"Yes," I replied.

Immediately detecting an issue concerning one of Mrs. Cohen's children, she shook her head knowingly. "If you have any trouble, tell me."

Knowing this woman believed in working on herself, I smiled my friendliest, least self-righteous, "we're all in this together" smile and asked, "Could that be *lashon hara* [derogatory or potentially harmful speech]?"

Startled, she became a bit defensive. "I don't think so. I was just trying to be helpful."

"I'm sure you were," I said kindly, "and I appreciate it, but I don't know if that was necessary to say."

A bit flustered, she responded, "Well, I don't know

if it was *lashon hara*," and retreated into her apartment.

Later, she called me. "I apologize," she said. "You were right. I'm really going to watch myself from now on."

I was impressed. *When your ego is healthy, you don't always need to protect it.*

Self-esteem attracts someone capable not only of healthy interactions, but of loving you for who you are. If you're not sure of yourself inside, you'll seek validation outside, based on how you look, where you've been, or what you can do. And this weakness will inevitably leave you, as an old song put it, "looking for love in all the wrong places."

A young woman told me unhappily that she kept getting involved with the wrong guys. She didn't want to, but some inner void compelled her—and with each episode she felt emptier. Although I knew she'd need counseling to work through this issue, I decided to take a guess at what might be going on.

"Do you think you got enough love from your parents—particularly your father?" I asked her point-blank. "Could that be why you're so hungry for male attention?"

Something dawned in her eyes. "It could be," she said slowly.

"Do your relationships give you the love you want?"

There was a long silence. "No—but for a while, they make me feel good."

"About who you are on the outside, or on the inside?"

There was a *very* long, painful silence. "Not the inside."

"Well," I said gently, "probably the best way to get the love you're looking for is to learn to love yourself."

A strong self-image protects you from self-destructive entanglements. It gives you the confidence to choose whom to be with, to believe someone worthwhile will choose you, and to settle for no less. Healthy self-esteem is a prerequisite of a healthy relationship. (For more on self-definition and self-esteem, see my book *Outside/Inside*.)

If self-esteem means believing in yourself, *trust* means believing in others. Like self-esteem, your ability to trust stems largely from your childhood, as well as from later relationships, which we often interpret in light of our growing-up experiences. If your parents were consistently there for you, you'll find it easier to trust, whereas if they were physically and/or emotionally unavailable, you'll suspect everyone.

Aliza had been waiting 25 minutes when Jason, whom she'd been dating several weeks, finally came running up. "Where were you?" she demanded. "You're late!"

"I'm so sorry," he panted, "but I missed the bus, and the next one took a long time to come, and—"

"That's no excuse!" she interrupted, her voice on the rise. "I've been waiting half an hour!"

Jason was upset. "Look, it's the first time this has happened, and I'll do my best not to let it happen again. I apologize."

On the verge of tears, Aliza barely registered his words. "I said I've been waiting *half an hour*! How do you think it feels, *wondering if you're even coming*?"

This young woman's distrust, undoubtedly rooted in her upbringing, will inevitably plague her marriage. Trust can also be damaged by even one traumatic breakup, including your parents' divorce (or worse, your own). If your trust level isn't where it should be, start giving it your attention (perhaps with a counselor). While a committed, loving relationship can build trust, you must have enough of it to get into one in the first place.

Self-esteem and trust lay the foundation for *emotional intimacy*. Intimacy is often confused with the intensity of a relationship's initial "Velcro" stage. Yet intimacy is not the sudden, illusory closeness that comes from strong chemistry, physical involvement, or the sensation of the walls between you and another tumbling down. Walls can be rebuilt in seconds, physical involvement may be only physical, and chemistry can backfire (see Chapter 3), converting "closeness" into distance. Intimacy is the ability to expose your inner self, be vulnerable, and let your partner do the same.

After two dates with Shari, Oren was enraptured. Shari always focused intently on him, gazing warmly into his eyes and displaying great interest in everything he said. Her voice was soft and gentle, her smile understanding. "I already feel so close to her," he sighed to his friend. "It's as if she *knows* me." While Shari made Ron feel special, that's not intimacy. Besides trust in another and belief in yourself, intimacy requires *really* knowing each other—and that takes time. *There are no shortcuts to intimacy.*

As with maturity and self-esteem, you will unconsciously be attracted to someone whose capacity for emotional intimacy matches your own.

Denise sought premarital counseling because she was frustrated that Ron seemed to blocked in developing greater closeness.

"When did you sense this about Ron?" the counselor asked.

"In the beginning of the relationship," she said sadly, "but I thought that with time he'd open up."

The counselor turned to Ron. "Let me ask you: How capable of genuine closeness do you feel Denise is?"

He hesitated. "Well, I've never told her this... but I think she's just as blocked as she says I am."

Denise was shocked. But she eventually realized that, as much as she craved intimacy, she also feared it, and that she'd unconsciously chosen Ron partly because he wouldn't push beyond her limits.

Even if your self-esteem and trust are solid, emotional intimacy may be difficult if your parents repressed their feelings, or if you "learned" not to express your own. While this problem may lack serious consequences until you're married, you may want to start looking at it now. Prying yourself open requires courage, but few kinds of growth are as rewarding, for emotional intimacy is not only the essence of marriage but one of life's most beautiful gifts. Unlocking your heart will feel like emerging from a dark closet into the sunshine, and it's easier to find your soulmate in the light.

Exploring these aspects of yourself may be a bit scary. But keep in mind: *People want to marry some-*

one as "together" as they are. I knew a woman who preferred not to delve into herself, until she inquired about a man she was interested in, and was told very deliberately, "He's not such a healthy, whole person, but that may be the best you can get right now." That gave her the impetus to start working on herself. Nearly all of us have issues—and it's worth looking into them before dating for marriage.

Know Yourself

Until now, I've discussed what you need to be a good partner for someone. Choosing the *right* someone requires even more self-knowledge. Ideally, one or more mentors can help clarify who you are and what you need in a spouse.

First, look at your nature. What are your strengths and weaknesses? What can you contribute to a relationship? What must your partner provide?

"My spirituality is a very people-oriented," I told my husband-to-be when we were dating. "I feel closest to God through how I relate to others." Avraham, I soon discovered, was very connected to the holidays and prayer. Together, our religious life is rich in all these elements. Your partner needn't be everything you're not, but it's wise to make sure the most important bases are covered. (Someone, for example, had better pay the bills.)

Next, understand your needs. This task is trickier, because it can be difficult to distinguish needs from wants. Needs are essential for your happiness and fulfillment. For instance, everyone needs various levels of emotional sharing, intellectual communication, joint religious observance, and material comfort. Wants, on the other hand, derive not from your deepest depths, but usually from peers, society, or the media. To differentiate needs from wants, you must strive to tune out these external voices.

Sherry spent several futile years looking for Mr. Perfect. Once she started listening to her inner self, however, she discovered that while she might *want* the personal ads' dream of a "tall, handsome, financially successful Renaissance man to share fine dining, exotic vacations, and romantic evenings by the fireside," what she *needed* was a reasonably attractive, intelligent mensch who'd make a decent living, encourage her career, love her, and want to grow spiritually and emotionally. She found him, and they're now happily married—so happily, in fact, that she's all but forgotten what she once sought.

Separating wants from needs is particularly important when they contradict. You may *want* a high-powered professional but may *need* someone more focused on spirituality; you may *want* an up-and-coming Torah scholar but *need* a husband who'll be free to spend a lot of time with you. Even when they don't clash, wants are the icing on the cake; needs are what count.

After needs, consider your values. Most of us passively assimilate those of society (which are often questionable), or choose from a limited range of options. How consciously and knowledgeably have you arrived at your values? While they may shift with time, you want to do enough searching and thinking to know what's important to you, and that it's unlikely to change, so your marriage will have a durable foundation. If you're newly religious, realize that integrating new beliefs and practices doesn't happen overnight. No matter how sure you are about your new direction, let it sink in and become part of you before involving yourself with someone.

Andy had been studying in an introductory program on Judaism when he met Deborah, who'd become observant a few years earlier. Within two weeks, a relationship had taken off, and Andy was certain he wanted to marry her. Deborah promised to wait for him while he "caught up" religiously, so Andy enrolled in yeshiva for half a year. They then wed. A year later they were divorced. "I really loved her—I still do—but I just wasn't ready to be religious," Andy confessed. "Deborah has beautiful hair and I didn't want her covering it. And I wasn't willing to stop doing everything I used to do on Saturdays. It was too much too fast. I felt trapped—and I had to get out."

Bringing Judaism into your life takes time. Whenever a young woman who's been observant all of six months excitedly informs me that she plans to start dating, my usual response is *"Hooold onnn!"*

While some people jump into religion too quickly, others don't pursue it enough before marriage. Carrie had studied in a beginners' program for a few weeks and become nominally observant. Eager to "move on," she married a fellow participant shortly afterwards. Now she wanted to become more religious, but her husband didn't. "I don't get it," she announced unhappily. "Isn't Jewish marriage supposed to be about spiritual growth?" It is. But before marrying, you must learn how you want to grow, so you'll know whom to grow with.

Finally, look more deeply into yourself. How has your upbringing shaped your personality and feelings? What unspoken emotional needs will you bring to a relationship? What are you unconsciously expecting of marriage?

These complicated matters are the topic of the next chapter.

Chapter Three
Behind the "Click"

You've learned about the personal qualities necessary for a healthy relationship, and I've encouraged you to strengthen them in yourself. In the next chapter, I'll share some wisdom about love and marriage which I hope you'll take to heart. Altogether, these will take you a long way toward readiness for a permanent relationship. Yet depending on the type of union you want, you may benefit from an additional kind of knowledge and growth.

Most of us choose a mate based on reason and emotion. Some work more intellectually, emphasizing objective criteria such as similar values and goals. Others follow their hearts, opting for someone who ignites certain feelings. Still others try to strike a balance. (In Chapter 6, I argue for leading with your head.) In the end, however, we're all looking for the ideological and personal compatibility that creates a strong connection.

Yet some individuals—and you may be one of them—want something more. Beneath it all (whether they admit it or not), they crave that indefinable, elusive "click."

After the fact, this "click" is often partly traceable to physical attraction, personal appeal, charisma, or a mixture. At the same time, most people will tell you "there's just something there," some inexplicable ingredient that makes the relationship feel right—and it's romantic to leave it a mystery. But if you're seeking this sensation, you may be interested in psychology's perspective. For it appears that the "click" originates not in anything mystical, but in your unconscious.

Being Human

According to a famous midrash (an ancient insight into the Bible), man and woman were created as one, after which God separated them into two incomplete beings. Unmarried males and females "remember" once being part of a whole and long to re-achieve oneness through reunion with their soulmates. We look to marriage to regain spiritual wholeness.

Psychology suggests another aspect of our incompleteness. Growing up, we acquired "defects." None of us reached adulthood in perfect emotional shape. Our psyche consequently wants to "fix things up." And just as we expect marriage to restore our spiritual wholeness, we often hope it will restore our emotional wholeness as well.

What is "emotional wholeness"? It's being completely joyful and relaxed, conscious of and connected to all aspects of your being—feeling totally loved, in touch with your whole self and fully alive.

If this description sounds like a dream, *it is*. Nobody makes it to adulthood "whole." However devoted and conscientious our parents or other caretakers may have been, they were human. They weren't all-knowing or all-powerful. In addition, they undoubtedly had their own emotional issues, which "leaked" into the way they raised us. Consequently, they couldn't give us all the nourishment we needed at every stage. We may have been criticized too often, had our feelings discounted, been given too much freedom or too little affection. In the end, these mistakes left us wanting.

Our parents may also have communicated discomfort with aspects of ourselves—perhaps our need to cry, dance, or state our opinions. Accordingly, we learned to repress and disown these features.

So, as normal human beings, our growing-up years weren't perfect. And while we may have emerged reasonably "together," we also emerged less than whole. (As a parent, I like to believe God gave me flaws so my kids will have "stuff" to work on as adults. I prefer seeing myself as the creator of their growth opportunities rather than as the one who messed them up.)

That we reached adulthood with some deficits could be the end of the story, if not for how we perceived reality in our earlier years. As small children, we tended to assume that most things—whether good or bad—happened because of us. (A child can believe that she caused her parents' divorce, or that she can reconcile them.) At the same time, we idolized our parents, believing anything they did must be right. For both these reasons, we couldn't recognize our parents' shortcomings and how they affected us. Instead, we unconsciously concluded that if they didn't give us all we needed, it must be our fault. We must not be fully deserving of love.

Feeling unlovable is painful. It's hard to live with. So our minds did us a huge favor: they stored this hurt out of reach, in our unconscious. And it's still there.

Most of us don't realize we're hurt. Whatever

"damage" we suffered may not noticeably affect our friendships, work or other activities, or keep us from happiness and success. Occasionally a seemingly insignificant event will provoke an unexplainable emotional reaction (which indicates it's "pushed a button" in our unconscious), but the feeling passes and life goes on.

Yet our hurts may become highly relevant when we look for a marriage partner. The following theory doesn't describe everyone. Yet it has pinpointed a significant (or even the key) component in many attractions. And the idea is that people's hurts directly underlie the "click" they're seeking.

The Unconscious Connection

As I said, adults want wholeness and unconditional love—and the theory is that *you're drawn to a person who you sense can provide them*. When you meet someone, your subliminal scanners spring into action. They scrutinize and register the person's facial expressions, eye contact, body language, walk, talk, attitude, style, and behavior, all in order to determine whether or not he or she possesses very specific traits. For as unromantic as it sounds, you are often unknowingly searching for someone who resembles your parents.

People react differently to this theory. If you think your parents are the greatest, you may be delighted. If you don't get along with them—well, you may be less than delighted. In either case, the notion of "marrying your parents" may disturb your sense of adult autonomy, and you may not buy it.

"Daniel [or Daniella] is nothing like either of my

parents," you may object. "My parents are both busi-nesspeople, and Daniel's an artist. My parents are out-going, and Daniel is introverted. They're night and day."

But if you delve deeper, you may find startling similarities. Perhaps Daniel approaches his art with the same single-minded dedication your parents give their business. Maybe Daniella quietly communicates the same feelings your parents do loudly. In fact, at some point in their marriage, many people find them-selves telling their spouses, "I can't believe how much you're like my mother," or "You know, you're acting just like my father."

What lies behind this attraction?

On a simple level, we're drawn to what's familiar. If you're dating just for fun, someone exotic may attract you; but when you're looking for the "real thing," you'll inevitably gravitate toward what you "know" and are therefore comfortable with—and nothing feels more familiar than the personalities of the people who raised you.

This tendency can be quite advantageous. If your parents were basically happy, understanding, sup-portive, and affectionate, you'll immediately "warm up" to and connect with someone who radiates those same desirable qualities.

But it's more complicated. For your unconscious also seeks someone with your parents' *hurtful* traits. It wants you to marry a person not only who recalls the best of Mom and Dad, but with whom you can re-experience the same "issues" you had with them. In placing yourself back in familiar emotional territory, it reasons, you'll have a second chance to emerge with all your needs met. The kind of love you didn't get from your folks, you'll now get from your spouse. You'll feel whole. And you'll be able to confirm at last: "It isn't because of me that I didn't get everything I needed from my parents. I'm getting it now, from someone who feels just like them. I *am* completely worthy of love."

Typically, within a few dates of "clicking" with somebody, you'll notice parental flaws in him or her. They may even disturb you. But the unconscious is a powerful persuader. Dr. Jeff Auerbach (author of *How to Irritate the Ones You Love: A Concise, Practical Guide to the True Nature of Relationships*) reconstructs the internal dialogue:

> *Conscious*: "Why does s/he do that? It kind of upsets me. I'm not sure I want to deal with that in a spouse."

> *Unconscious*: "Are you kidding? This is *perfect*. This is exactly the right person to give you what you never got from your parents."

> *Conscious*: "Hmm. Actually, it's not such a big deal. And anyway, s/he has so many traits I really like."

And here's the dead giveaway that your unconscious is pulling the strings:

> *Conscious*: "And I can always get him/her to *change* [into who I wanted my parents to be]."

A friend of mine recounts a brief conversation with her future father-in-law. "I hope you know," he told her, "that my son rarely talks about his feelings."

"Oh, I'm used to that," she responded lightly. "My father was the same way."

She didn't realize that this was no coincidence—or that the scars of a less-than-perfect father-daughter relationship would underlie her struggle to get her husband to be more emotionally expressive.

In addition to a parental "feel-alike" who'll "do it right" this time, you seek a mate with whom you can vicariously experience repressed aspects of yourself. If you were raised to live in your head, you may be attracted to a very feeling person. If you were taught to always plan, you may be drawn to someone spontaneous. This desire to reclaim lost parts of ourselves is often why "opposites attract."

These are the main pieces in the attraction puzzle. A "click," in short, reflects the unconscious hope that the "clicker" will fix the mistakes of your childhood and make you whole. Without knowing your inner self, however, you won't realize that. Upon meeting the "wrong" person, your unconscious will quickly conclude: "Nope, nothing familiar here to fulfill my needs," while all you'll consciously think is "She's perfectly pretty, nice, and intelligent... still, I don't feel anything special." But when those subliminal scanners identify a winner, your unconscious will light up: "Yes! This one will make everything right!" while all you'll be aware of is "Wow—I really like him and we have a lot in common. I think there's potential here."

As you're experiencing all this unconscious activity, so is your partner. He too hopes you will heal his childhood hurts. She too believes you will make her feel whole and fully loved. Furthermore, to win each other over, each of you will deftly divine exactly what your partner wants and provide it. The result can be euphoria. For fueling your romance is the intoxicating feeling that, however much you missed or lost in childhood, *you're going to get it all back*. While simple physical attraction may make a young teenager's heart throb, this heady anticipation of feeling whole and worthy is what most adults call falling in love.

Wake-Up Time

If this kind of romance could continue, you'd live happily ever after, like in Walt Disney movies. But once you marry, the plot thickens. Whether after a week, a month, or a few months, you may wake up one morning and realize you're no longer in an enchanted world. And unless you're prepared, it can be a shock.

Jon and Rebecca can tell you about it. Two solidly grounded singles, each felt ready for marriage. Both had worked on themselves and tried to learn what they'd need to have a successful relationship. In addition, both came from emotionally healthy families headed by happily married parents. Like everyone, however, Jon and Rebecca's upbringings weren't perfect, and influenced their choice of whom to marry— and what happened after the wedding.

Jon grew up in a somewhat controlling environment. His mother was warm, bubbly, and loving but over-involved in his life. Whenever he came home, she'd ask where he'd been, what he'd done, and what he was planning next. Jon felt smothered and developed a strong need for space. His father was more relaxed. Bright and articulate, he shared most of his thoughts and feelings but had difficulty when it came to love. Jon too acquired an active mind and expressive personality but, like his father, was uneasy showing affection.

Rebecca's parents were similar to Jon's, yet different. Her father was highly intelligent but quite critical, often expressing his love only after she brought home a straight-A report card. Rebecca was left feeling that love depended upon approval, while, deep down, she hungered to be loved simply for who she was. Her mother was less judgmental. Gregarious and full of positive energy, she was nonetheless detached from many of her feelings. Like her, Rebecca developed an emotional, outgoing personality, but had trouble recognizing and expressing everything going on inside.

When Jon and Rebecca met, they "clicked" immediately. Rebecca was attracted to Jon's sharp mind and personality (which recalled her father), happily overlooking that he could sometimes be *too* sharp. Jon was drawn to Rebecca's exuberant interest in his life (much like his mother's), ignoring that it was sometimes *too* exuberant.

Then there were each other's "lost" traits. Jon's ease in speaking his mind was a breath of fresh air to Rebecca, helping her reconnect to the full range of her own emotions. Rebecca's open affection stirred something deep within Jon, putting him back in touch with his buried desire to express love.

Increasingly feeling "this is it," Jon and Rebecca made special efforts to fulfill each other's unspoken needs. Sensing that Jon wanted space, Rebecca let him volunteer information about his activities rather than questioning him. Aware that she craved total affirmation, Jon frequently told her how special she was and avoided any criticism. The result was wonderful. "It feels so right," Jon enthused to his roommate. "I can't believe how close I already feel to him," Rebecca marveled to her best friend. They were soon engaged and married.

Yet a few months later, things were no longer going so smoothly. Unconsciously, Rebecca had been counting on receiving the unconditional love she hadn't gotten from her father, while Jon had expected the emotional space his mother hadn't provided. But their wishes weren't being fulfilled. On the contrary, each person seemed to be hurting the other just as he or she had been hurt as a child. Jon's incisive thinking was sounding increasingly critical, re-igniting Rebecca's fear of not being loved. Rebecca's effusiveness was becoming overbearing, suffocating Jon again. Each person was touching the very nerves the other's parents had made raw. "Why has everything changed?" they wondered unhappily. As their disenchantment grew, each focused less on the other's needs and more on his or her own. Rebecca demanded more loving attention, while Jon insisted on more time to himself—which only made Rebecca more demanding, causing Jon to distance himself further. A vicious cycle had been set in motion.

Additional parts of each other's personalities, once welcomed, were now troubling them as well. Jon's readiness to express a wide range of emotions was beginning to disturb Rebecca (as her mother had "taught" her it should). Rebecca's affection was starting to embarrass Jon (as he had "learned" from his father). Parental messages of "we don't do this" resurfaced, and the very traits that had initially attracted them were now repelling them.

After only a few months of marriage, Jon and Rebecca were each wondering if their match was a mistake. Believe it or not, though, this turn of events is *normal*. Many successful marriages go through it. For while the "click" that brought Jon and Rebecca together has created difficulty, it also promises tremendous growth and fulfillment—*if* they each strive to understand why they were attracted, work to lighten their own emotional load, and reach out to nurture the other. God may even have created this "unconscious spouse choice" to encourage both marriage partners to confront their hurts and grow past them, so they can become more complete, not only as individuals, but as a couple.

With a lot of effort (and some counseling), Jon and Rebecca achieved a solid, happy relationship. At the same time, their journey to wholeness could have been easier had they each embarked upon it with greater self-awareness and a head start on the growth their marriage would require.

Becoming Aware

As the typical (and highly simplified) story above makes clear, major marital issues often stem from that initial "click." While numerous marriages fail due to lack of personal development and/or proper values, others dive-bomb because partners can't or won't get on top of, and beyond, what's unconsciously driving them and their relationship.

Of course, to avoid these conflicts, you can forgo

the "click." Shared goals and values, mutual respect and admiration, good communication, physical attraction, and enjoyment of each other's company can be quite enough to build a beautiful marriage. While the relationship may initially be less intense than an unconsciously chosen one, it can be every bit as good, and possibly easier. (I know a few individuals who'd do better with a mail-order bride or groom than with the partners they keep selecting.)

If you want a "click," however, prepare to deal with deeper issues. The solution—and the solution to most marital difficulties—will be to do all you can to fulfill your partner's emotional needs (assuming at least some reciprocity). Unconditional giving not only creates love (as you'll read in the next chapter), but helps heal childhood wounds. Yet it can be hard to give when you're blocked by feelings of mysterious origin.

What all this means for your marriage preparation is clear: You must approach marriage with a healthy realism and respect for its complexity—which may include getting to know yourself more deeply. As psychologist Harville Hendrix writes in *Getting the Love You Want* (a book whose "popular" title belies its content), "whether or not you realize the full potential [of an intimate, joyful, lifelong union] depends not on your ability to attract the perfect mate, but on your willingness to acquire knowledge about hidden parts of yourself." For while a good marriage can be healing, making you whole is not your spouse's responsibility—*it's your own*. By getting in touch with old hurts and emotional needs *before* you marry, you can reduce their intensity, and you'll bring less baggage and greater understanding to your relationship. And you'll more likely marry someone who, like you, is more whole.

To discover your inner self, you must examine your upbringing and how it affected you. Occasionally an insightful friend can help. For many of us, however, the quickest and most effective route is goal-oriented counseling by a professional experienced in helping singles prepare for marriage. Getting counseling doesn't mean you have a problem—it means you want a helping hand in learning how to live the happiest, most productive life possible. Any counselor you choose should be licensed, compatible with your personality, culture, and religious beliefs, and someone with whom you feel a connection. He or she should also quickly identify your issues and assist you in getting past them. Yes, it costs money, but it won't cost any less after you're married, when matters will be twice as complex. Considering how much people spend on a beautiful wedding, why not devote part of that sum to preparing for a great marriage?

Marriage takes root and blossoms in the soil of shared goals, respect, and appreciation. For some of us, its success also depends on resolving old issues and becoming more whole. With enough effort and inner work—and, as always, prayer—your marriage can be the deeply rewarding experience it is meant to be.

Part III
Being Wise

The foundation of any great marriage is *hashkafa* (outlook), meaning solid, well-thought-out values and a healthy direction. Chapter 4, "Love and Marriage," gives you some of the fundamental insight you'll need to have a successful relationship. Chapter 5, "Affirming Womanhood," addresses the often controversial issue of Jewish women and their role today.

Chapter Four
Love and Marriage

E ven if this chapter were a book in itself, it couldn't begin to capture all the dimensions of such a rich part of life as love and marriage. The topic is as vast as the sea. I hope the following basic ideas will launch a lifetime of learning.

The Gift of Love

A few years ago, I spoke to a group of high-schoolers from non-religious homes about the Jewish idea of love.

"Someone define love," I said.

No response.

"Doesn't anyone want to try?" I asked.

Still no response.

"Tell you what: I'll define it, and you raise your hands if you agree. Okay?"

Nods.

"Okay. Love is that feeling you get when you meet the right person."

Every hand went up. And I thought, *Oy*.

This is how many people approach a relationship. Consciously or unconsciously, they believe love is a sensation (based on physical and emotional attraction) that magically, spontaneously generates when Mr. or Ms. Right appears. And just as easily, it can spontaneously *de*generate when the magic "just isn't there" anymore. You fall in love, and you can fall out of it. The key word is *passivity*. Erich Fromm, in his famous treatise *The Art of Loving*, noted the sad consequence of this misconception: "There is hardly any activity, any enterprise, which is started with such tremendous hopes and expectations, and yet, which fails so regularly, as love." (That was back in 1956— chances are he'd be even more pessimistic today.)

So what is love—real, lasting love? *Love is the attachment that results from deeply appreciating another's goodness.*

The word "goodness" may surprise you. After all, most love stories don't feature a couple enraptured with each other's ethics. ("I'm captivated by your values!" he told her passionately. "And I've never met a man with such morals!" she cooed.) But in her study of real-life successful marriages (*The Good Marriage: How & Why Love Lasts*), Judith Wallerstein reports that "the value these couples placed on the partner's moral qualities was an unexpected finding." To the Jewish mind, it isn't unexpected at all. What we value most in ourselves, we value most in others. God created us to see ourselves as good (hence our need to either rationalize or regret our wrongdoings). So, too, we seek goodness in others. Nice looks, an engaging personality, intelligence, and talent (all of which count for something) may attract you, but goodness is what moves you to love.

If love comes from appreciating goodness, it needn't just happen—you can make it happen. Love is *active*. You can create it. Just focus on the good in another person (and everyone has some). If you can do this easily, you'll love easily.

I was once at an intimate concert in which the performer, a deeply spiritual person, gazed warmly at his audience and said, "I want you to know, I love you all." I smiled tolerantly and thought, "Sure." Looking back, though, I realize my cynicism was misplaced. This man naturally saw the good in others, and our being there said enough about us that he could love us. Judaism actually idealizes this universal, unconditional love.

Obviously, there's a huge distance from here to the far more profound, personal love developed over the years, especially in marriage. But seeing goodness is the beginning.

Susan learned about this foundation of love after becoming engaged to David. When she called her parents to tell them the good news, they were elated. At the end of the conversation, her mother said, "Darling, I want you to know we love you, and we love David."

Susan was a bit dubious. "Mom," she said hesitantly, "I really appreciate your feelings, but, in all honesty, how can you say you love someone you've never met?"

"We're *choosing* to love him," her mother explained, "because *love is a choice*."

There's no better wisdom Susan's mother could have imparted to her before marriage. By focusing on the good, you can love almost anyone.

Now that you're feeling so warmly toward the entire human race, how can you deepen your love for someone? The way God created us, actions affect our feelings most. For example, if you want to become more compassionate, thinking compassionate thoughts may be a start, but giving *tzedaka* (charity) will get you there. Likewise, the best way to *feel* loving is to *be* loving—and that means *giving*. While most people believe love leads to giving, the truth (as Rabbi Eliyahu Dessler writes in *Kuntres HaChesed*, his famous discourse on lovingkindness) is exactly the opposite: Giving leads to love.

What is giving? When an enthusiastic handyman happily announces to his non-mechanically inclined wife, "Honey, wait till you see what I got you for your birthday—a triple-decker toolbox!" that's not giving. Neither is a parent's forcing violin lessons on his son because he himself always dreamed of being a virtuoso. True giving, as Erich Fromm points out, is *other-oriented*, and requires four elements. The first is *care*, demonstrating active concern for the recipient's life and growth. The second is *responsibility*, responding to his or her expressed and unexpressed needs (particularly, in an adult relationship, emotional needs). The third is *respect*, "the ability to see a person as he [or she] is, to be aware of his [or her] unique individuality," and, consequently, wanting that person to "grow and unfold as he [or she] is." These three components all depend upon the fourth, *knowledge*. You can care for, respond to, and respect another only as deeply as you know him or her.

The effect of genuine, other-oriented giving is profound. It allows you into another person's world and opens you up to perceiving his or her goodness. At the same time, it means investing part of yourself in the other, enabling you to love this person as you love yourself.

Many years ago, I met a woman whom I found very unpleasant. So I decided to try out the "giving leads to love" theory. One day I invited her for dinner. A few days later I offered to help her with a personal problem. On another occasion I read something she'd written and offered feedback and praise. Today we have a warm relationship. The more you give, the more you love. This is why your parents (who've given you more than you'll ever know) undoubtedly love you more than you love them, and you, in turn, will love your own children more than they'll love you.

Because deep, intimate love emanates from knowledge and giving, it comes not overnight but over time—which nearly always means after marriage. The intensity many couples feel before marrying is usually great affection boosted by commonality, chemistry, and anticipation. These may be the seeds of love, but they have yet to sprout. On the wedding day, emotions run high, but true love should be at its lowest, because it will hopefully always be growing, as husband and wife give more and more to each other.

A woman I know once explained why she's been happily married for twenty-five years. "A relationship has its ups and downs," she told me. "The downs can be really low—and when you're in one, you have three choices: Leave, stay in a loveless marriage, or choose to love your spouse." Dr. Jill Murray (author of *But I Love Him: Protecting Your Daughter from Controlling, Abusive Dating Relationships*) writes that if someone mistreats you while professing to love you, remember: *"Love is a behavior."* A relationship thrives when partners are committed to behaving lovingly through continual, unconditional giving—not only saying "I love you," but showing it.

Unfortunately, giving doesn't always come easily. In a self-centered society, looking out for yourself can seem like a virtue, whereas giving too readily means risking being taken advantage of. Women, more giving by nature, can be particularly wary of this danger. After eating a Shabbat meal at someone's house, a certain young woman was asked to help clean up. Defensively, she snapped, "I don't do dishes." (I used to be tempted to respond similarly if the men weren't helping, until I decided that their not being menschen wouldn't keep me from being one.) Chances are such a woman will fear being a doormat in her marriage as well. Yet "looking out for Number One" isn't necessary if each partner is committed to looking out for the other.

Here's how Rabbi Shmuel Veffer, teaching on the Discovery program in Jerusalem, illustrated it:

You and your spouse have worked hard this year. You now have the opportunity to take a long-awaited vacation together, and you're deciding how to spend it.

"I feel so restless after being in that office forty hours a week," you complain. "How about going up to the mountains for some hiking and camping?"

"That's a vacation?" your spouse groans. "After chasing two little kids all day, I just want to stretch out on a lawn chair and recuperate."

"I've been sitting at a desk for months, and now I have to be a couch potato? I want to get out there, get moving, be active."

"Walking from my hotel room to the pool and back is more than enough activity for me."

In the end, the two of you compromise on a lakeside cabin. But the negativity your selfishness has generated has ruined your vacation—and worse, you've moved farther apart.

But it could have been different:

"You seem worn out," you tell your spouse sympathetically. "Maybe we should go to a nice, restful resort."

"That sounds wonderful," he or she replies, "but after so much time in the office, you probably need to get out and get moving. Why don't we do some hiking and camping?"

"That would be fun, but wouldn't it be too much for you? I think we should go someplace where you can relax."

"You'd be unhappy sitting around like that. Let's do something more active."

In the end, the two of you compromise on a lakeside cabin. But you're happy and charged with positive energy toward each other. More important, you've taken a giant step toward building your love by asking not "What's in it for me?" but "What's in it for you?"

Yet giving that creates love also demands an identity of your own, integrity, and. awareness of your needs. (That's what prevents you from being taken advantage of.) Genuine love emerges not from lack of self but from a desire to share all you are with another. Riding in a taxi recently, I heard a popular song on Israeli radio. "With you, I'm the whole world; with you, I'm the whole universe," the male singer crooned. "Without you, I'm only half a person; without you, I'm actually nothing." Ugh, I thought—that's not love, that's neurosis. (And, wincing, I wondered how many teenage girls are dying to have a guy sing that to them.) "Losing yourself" in a relationship, furthermore, requires a partner who's doing the same or, alternatively, who's content to let you do all the giving. Neither scenario is good. *Healthy* giving includes reciprocity (barring unusual circumstances) and stems from a solid sense of self. In a healthy relationship, rather than losing yourself, you find yourself.

Besides knowing what love is, it helps to know what it isn't. Love is not a panacea. It won't give you identity, meaning, or purpose. It (alone) won't make you a better person. And it won't make you perfectly happy. A relationship with another person can never do these things—only a relationship with God can. In addition, love won't make you emotionally whole. It won't rescue you from change or remove pain. It may even augment it until you and your partner work through your issues. Finally, love isn't "dramatic," at least not in the conventional sense of the word.

Love can, however, help you feel centered and at home in the world, inspire growth, and contribute significantly to happiness. With the right kind of work, it can heal. And while love has excitement and passion, there's even greater pleasure in the quiet drama of two souls moving closer. This deeply peaceful sense of increasing oneness is perhaps the most wonderful reward of love.

The Road to Oneness

Marriage is the framework in which love can develop. As the ultimate union of souls, a good marriage cultivates powerful and unparalleled feelings of belonging, fulfillment, and completion. That this supreme mitzvah (commandment) offers such deep satisfaction is one of God's most wonderful gifts.

Yet marriage, like love, is riddled with false expectations. These are rooted partly in the frequent, unconscious hope that marriage will make up for one's childhood (as discussed in Chapter 3). They also stem from the media, which sells relationships—and life itself—as an endless merry-go-round of passion and fun. And, of course, there's that age-old fairy tale ending, which we dismiss intellectually yet cling to in our dreams: "And they lived happily ever after." (I avoid reading my children such stories; I prefer ones like *The Paper Bag Princess*, in which, after outwitting a dragon and rescuing her beloved prince, the princess realizes the latter is a bum, and they don't get married after all. Anything is more realistic than "happily ever after.")

So if marriage isn't the dream it's made out to be, what is it? Like love, it is far more grounded and real, yet lofty: *Marriage is the spiritual union of two people who want to share their lives and achieve common goals.*

"Achieving common goals" may sound about as romantic as a business partnership. But these goals are profound. They include love, spiritual and emotional growth, and oneness with your spouse.

At the same time, marriage is larger than your personal relationship. In an article entitled "The End of Courtship" (*The Public Interest*, Winter 1997), writer Leon Kass attributes marital failure to, among other factors, "an ethos that lacks transcendent aspirations." A marriage focused solely on feeling good together is bound to suffer, because it can never provide the ongoing, emotional back-rub many expect. When you live for something beyond your own happiness—such as building a family, being part of a community, and contributing to others (all part of serving God)—personal issues are less likely to overwhelm and destroy the relationship.

This is not to say you shouldn't be happy. But happiness in marriage, as in life, is not a goal; it's a by-product. It cannot be pursued directly; it comes from doing what your true self wants. When you use what God has given you to give to others, you're happy. When you and your partner give to each other in the framework of goals that both include and transcend the two of you, you're a happy couple.

Goal-oriented marriage takes time and patience. I remember being married three months and wondering, "If husband and wife are supposed to be so close, how come part of me still feels closer to my old roommate?" Somehow I didn't realize I wouldn't bond deeply with my husband right away. As much as you may long for it, marriage is not an "arrival." It is the beginning of a long process of building something together, whose rewards come not at the end but every step along the way.

Achieving goals requires effort. This should go without saying, but many adults throw in the towel as soon as things stop feeling good. I know a woman whose husband told her, shortly after their wedding, "Well, it doesn't seem to be working, so I guess we should get divorced"—and they did. Even the best relationship has conflicts and dissatisfactions, but both partners invest in resolving them amid caring and connection. *It's through working past problems that a marriage becomes beautiful.*

The fact that marriage takes work implies that your spouse will be neither perfect nor perfectly compatible with you. (The latter is guaranteed by, if nothing else, the fact that one of you is male and the other female.) *A spouse is not a fantasy fulfillment.* I asked the same group of teenagers who believed love is a feeling you get, "How many of you expect the person you marry to satisfy all your emotional needs?" Again every hand went up—and again I thought, *Oy.* Your mate should share your perspective on life's most important issues and become your most intimate companion. But unless he or she wears a shirt emblazoned with a big, red "S" and can leap tall buildings in a single bound, don't expect *everything.* You may have to turn to teachers for high-level intellectual stimulation and to same-sex friends for understanding on issues your spouse (despite his or her best efforts) can't relate to. Likewise, your partner will not be Superman or Superwoman in Torah study, career, or cooking. Nor will he or she look like a supermodel. (Without a ton of make-up, lighting, and airbrushing, even supermodels don't look like supermodels.) None of this means you married the wrong person. It means you married a human, *like yourself.* Your spouse won't be any more perfect than you are, but as your soulmate (see the end of Chapter 5), your spouse will be perfect for *you.*

Marriage, therefore, is based on realism—and one thing that can destroy it is the media. The worst offender is television. The problem is not just what we're shown—beautiful couples whose problems are solved in half an hour of prime time—but the medium itself. Television by nature is suited only for bold, coarse, shallow, fast-paced action; any show attempting to depict anything quiet, subtle, gradual, or profound—like the development of a deep relationship over many years—would put us to sleep. This limitation makes television distinctly anti-reality, which also means anti-love and anti-marriage. With a lot of viewing, we begin perceiving relationships superficially. (I recall a comic scene in the movie *Being There*, in which a lonely gardener, whose knowledge of the outside world comes only from TV, tries to romance a woman, but he can only go through the motions. There's no content. It's extreme, but there's a message there.) If you're serious about approaching love and marriage with the healthiest mindset possible, spend less time in front of the TV and more time in the real world, where real relationships take place. (I stopped watching TV at age 18, after a book called *Four Arguments for the Elimination of Televison* by Jerry Mander convinced me I no longer wanted it in my system. It was one of the best things I could have done for my future marriage.)

While you choose how much television to watch, you have no choice about other influences on your marriage, such as your parents' relationship. A bad marriage or divorce may have wreaked havoc on your family (and, as with any childhood trauma, it's worth working through your feelings with a qualified counselor). But you are by no means doomed to your parents' fate, if you prepare for your own relationship and work on it once you're in it. In *The Good Marriage*, most of the happily married couples interviewed perceived their parents' marriages as *un*happy. By the same token, if your parents' marriage is successful, don't assume you'll naturally follow in their footsteps; plenty of people from intact homes have become divorce statistics. While your past affects your future, it doesn't determine it—God and you do. Choosing wisdom and growth will empower you, with God's help, to create the marriage you want.

Just like love, a good marriage is something you make happen. *Your personal development and willingness to work will affect your success far more than whomever you marry.* As a rabbi I know puts it, "What makes a marriage work? The *skills* to make it work." Giving, communication, respect, the desire to grow—these are the building blocks of a solid, happy union.

The most defining aspect of a successful, lifelong relationship is oneness between husband and wife. Oneness means seeing yourselves as a single unit, with each party acting and feeling in tandem with the other. In addition to love and emotional intimacy, one thing crucial to fostering oneness is *exclusivity*. Exclusivity means erecting the boundaries necessary to preserve the privacy and specialness of your relationship.

Fran was friendly with Craig when she met her husband-to-be. Now she's married, and she's redefined that old relationship: "*I'm* no longer friends with Craig—*my husband and I* are friends with Craig. I'm part of a couple, and I don't want a male friendship independent of my husband. I've stepped back emotionally as well. My husband isn't jealous or insecure—things just feel healthier this way. It was a little hard for Craig at first, but he's come to understand."

Particularly in your interactions with the opposite sex, every healthy line you draw ("We can be friendly to this degree, but no more") is an act of love for your spouse, making your marriage into a sanctified space, reserved only for the two of you.

The essence of oneness, however, is *mutual identification*. This means seeing your spouse as part of you, sharing her pains (as the saintly Rabbi Aryeh Levine told a doctor, "My wife's foot hurts us") and his joys. It means recognizing that hurting him is hurting yourself, while nurturing her is nurturing yourself. Such is the commitment of marriage. Or better, as *Shmooze: A Guide to Thought-Provoking Discussions on Essential Jewish Issues* puts it: "I'm not committed to my hand; I am my hand, and my hand is me." And just as nothing short of gangrene would cause you to amputate a limb, only something grave and incurable would prompt you to terminate your commitment to your spouse.

Mutual identification also means sacrificing some of your independence and desires for the sake of your union. I know a man whose business takes him overseas frequently. His wife is terribly lonely, but he loves his work and refuses to change jobs. This is not a marriage. Just as dancing requires synchronization, marriage means making every move with your partner's happiness in mind.

Once you marry and become one, however, neither of you disappears. A "we" is built on two "I"s, not two nobodies. Who you each continue to be and what you contribute as individuals is what gives your oneness its strength. At the same time, inclusion in that greater whole makes each of you far more than what you were.

Despite all its realism, then, marriage is somewhat supernatural. Its formula is not one plus one equals two, or two halves equal a whole. It's one plus one equals One. It's like overlapping red and blue to create purple and seeing all three colors simultaneously: each of your personalities plus your shared destiny.

All in all, love and marriage are a spiritual journey calling for change and growth, so embark upon it with wisdom. Though the ride may at times be bumpy, if you know your destination and are willing to work your way there, the trek can be deeply rewarding.

Chapter Five
*Affirming Womanhood**

W hen I was single and newly religious, a topic of much discussion among my peers was gender roles in marriage. Seeking input, my friend Shira asked an intelligent, religious wife and mother of several young children how she approached the issue.

"I run our home on my own," the woman told her. "That frees my husband to devote all his time to studying and teaching."

Shira had hoped for a different response. "I'm into traditionally feminine stuff," she said, "but I could never live with such a black-and-white role division. I have too many intellectual needs that can't be met through homemaking and caring for children. And I don't want a babysitter to raise my kids. So I need a husband who'll be more involved at home."

The woman shook her head. "Neither you nor your husband will reach your potential by being a jack-of-all-trades. To excel, you have to specialize. Your husband should have his realm, and you should have yours."

Shira left depressed. "It kind of makes sense," she later admitted, "but what if your personal reality doesn't fit?"

Shira married a man with whom she could build the life she wanted. Nevertheless, she was haunted by the traditional ideal of full-time homemaking, or at

---

*Note: This chapter is *not* only for women.

least working so her husband could study Torah. For a long time, she alternated between feeling inadequate and resenting those feelings.

Robin was a stay-at-home mom to two small children when her husband, a professor of Jewish studies, brought the family to Israel for a sabbatical. She stopped by for a visit, looking unhappy. "I don't think my husband respects me," she told me. "He sees this year as a opportunity for intellectual development and is always attending classes. I go to some as well, but after an hour or two I'm ready to return home to my kids."

"So what's the problem?"

"Well, I wouldn't have thought there was one, but my husband does. The other day he asked me, 'Don't you want to do something more with your life? Don't you want to grow?' But I love reading my children new books, baking cookies with them, teaching them Hebrew, and playing with them—and I feel I *am* growing from being a full-time mother."

She looked at me sadly. "I used to feel fine about myself, but lately I've been wondering—am I missing something?"

Not all Jewish women face these dilemmas. Some embrace domesticity. Others sidestep it. Still others balance homemaking and career to their satisfaction. But with both secular and Jewish society issuing loud and often self-contradictory messages about who women should be, many are confused.

Male or female, your feelings about the role of the Jewish woman will greatly affect whom you marry, the relationship the two of you build, and the rewards marriage and family bring you. So wherever you stand regarding tradition, the following perspective on Jewish womanhood may help you appreciate—and if necessary, negotiate—the often conflicting needs of women today.

Tradition*

What do Judaism and Jewish tradition say about women and their purpose in the world?

The Torah introduces the creation of woman with a verse: "And the Lord God said, It is not good that Adam should be alone; I will make him a help to match him" (Genesis 2:18). Woman is conceived to help man. Being someone's "helper" conjures up all those unpleasant "sub" words—submissive, subservient, subordinate, subjugated—which imply inferiority.

But is this really what "helping" means?

Take the biggest Helper of all: God. God is not inferior. If you've ever made a request of God, it's because you realize God can help you, and you need help. Similarly, defining woman as man's helper doesn't place her beneath him. It just means that woman can help man more than he can help her, whereas man is more in need of help. And just as God's being a "helper" doesn't make God less important than you, a woman who contributes equally to what she and her husband are working to achieve is no less important than he.

Furthermore, "helper" doesn't mean "servant." A servant obeys orders; a helper tries to do what's best

---

*I credit my teacher Rebbetzin Tziporah Heller for the fundamental understanding of women presented in this section ("Tradition").

for the "helpee." The Hebrew word "to match him" (*kenegdo*) literally means "opposite him." Woman is to stand opposite man, viewing him from her own vantage point and deciding how to help him—sometimes even by opposing him.

What kind of help was woman created to provide? In the Garden of Eden, man and woman had virtually no physical needs. They didn't wear clothing, and food grew ready-to-eat. With no work, man didn't need a housekeeper or a secretary. The only help woman could offer was *spiritual* help. After the fatal mistake of eating from the Tree of Knowledge of Good and Evil, when man was cursed with physical toil, one could argue that woman's helping role was extended to the material realm, such as cooking the food he labors to grow (or today, to buy). But her reason for existence, and the essential help she provides, remains spiritual.

Still, since woman is man's helper, if there were no men, would there be no need for women? The answer to this question, expressed in a well-known midrash, leads us to a far deeper understanding of woman's role.

When we were slaves in Egypt, the Torah tells us, Pharaoh decreed that all newborn male babies be drowned in the Nile. The midrash (*Yalkut Shimoni*, Shemot 2:165) recounts that our leader, Amram, resolved to bring no more children into such a world, so he divorced his wife Yocheved. The rest of the male Israelite population followed suit. But Amram's 5-year-old Miriam rebuked her father. "What you've done is worse than what Pharaoh's done," she told him. "Pharaoh has decreed death upon all baby boys, but you, by refusing to father more children, have terminated all future generations of girls as well."

Amram could have responded, "So what? With no more males, why do we need females?" But he didn't; he promptly remarried his wife, and the rest of the men did likewise. And from Amram's reunion with Yocheved came Moshe (Moses), who led us out of Egypt and brought us to Mount Sinai to receive the Torah. Amram understood Miriam's implicit message: that *women are valuable in and of themselves*. And our redemption and emergence as God's nation sprang from that affirmation of intrinsic female worth.

Of course, a woman's value may reveal itself indirectly through her effect on others. I know a childless woman who fostered countless physically and mentally challenged youngsters—as many as seven at a time. If you met her, she might not seem so special. And she wants it that way. But each child she nurtured is a powerful testament to her quiet strength and inner greatness.

So besides helping man, woman has her own reason to be. Perhaps women are to assist in a cosmic sense, to contribute something we *all* need. Indeed, "Adam," the beneficiary of woman's help, is midrashically understood not as "man" but as humankind. So how do women aid humanity?

Woman, the Torah tells us, was built from man's rib. The rib protects the vital organs while remaining invisible to the outside. This symbolism suggests that women are to safeguard spirituality by maintaining consciousness of the unseen and internal.

There's a lot to be said for concealment. The invisible is always more powerful. The best example, again, is God. The One who brought the whole cosmos into existence, sustains it every moment, and is intimately involved in every aspect of our lives is totally unseen. And while God is outside of and beyond us, we all possess a part of God within us—our *neshama* (soul). Our most enduring and real self, and the driving force behind our greatest accomplishments, is unseen and inside.

How does a woman express her special relationship to the internal?

The cornerstone of this connection, and woman's trademark, is *tzniut*. Inadequately translated as modesty, *tzniut* is not only a dress and behavior code. In fact, few of us deeply understand it.

Tzniut, related to the word *tzin'a*, privacy, is a consciousness translated into action. It starts with the recognition that your source of uniqueness and self-worth is not your looks, accomplishments, talents, or anything else you can see. Your true identity is who you are inside—your ability to approach God by becoming a better human being. *Tzniut* then means knowing when and how to keep your outside private, reflecting your inner self rather than outshining it.

I read a story in which a group of women set up a female friend, a professor, on a blind date. They warned the man that, as a bookish intellectual, she might dress very conservatively. Instead, she showed up in a low-cut blouse and a skirt with a thigh-high slit. "Wow!" her date exclaimed. "Your brains don't show at all!"

Society is increasingly obsessed with externals. We devote more energy to appearance than to essence.

Tzniut asks us to focus on the latter—which, even more than your brains, is your *neshama*. When we're undistracted by body or behavior, it's easier to see what lies beneath. Dressing and acting with *tzniut* challenges others to look past your outside to your inside and encourages you to appreciate who you really are.

The Midrash states that upon creating woman, God told her, *"Tehe isha tznua"*—"Be a woman who defines herself internally" (*Bereshit Rabba* 18:2). *Tzniut* is a virtue for both sexes, but women are its special guardian. (For a fuller discussion of the deeper meaning of *tzniut*, see my book *Outside/Inside*.)

A second significant expression of womanhood, strongly connected to *tzniut*, is homemaking. Homemaking means creating a nurturing environment for the inner self. Much of our lives takes place in public, where we often must don a uniform and be rated by external criteria, such as appearance or performance. Judaism sees women as gifted with the emotional skills necessary to build a home, a private sanctuary in which you can return to yourself.

Like most occupations today, homemaking has been stripped of its spiritual content. Yet the consequences for homemaking have been particularly severe. When you despiritualize medicine or law, you still have an interesting profession ringing with intelligence and ambition. But when you take the spirituality out of homemaking, you're left with housekeeping, which many find exceptionally brainless and boring. Making a home, however, doesn't necessarily mean being the one who cleans it. Making a home means creating a place that nourishes body and soul.

Homemaking also suffers from an absence of income and public recognition. Yet neither of these indicate spiritual worth. A top basketball star earns several million dollars a year, while those who saved lives during the Holocaust received no reimbursement. Nor do homemakers. The most meaningful jobs don't come with a salary (or at least not a significant one). Nor do they necessarily make one famous. As Rabbi Nachum Braverman (author of *The Death of Cupid: Reclaiming the Wisdom of Love, Dating, Romance and Marriage*) once wrote, Mother Theresa may have won the Nobel Prize for caring for the sick, dirty, and helpless in Calcutta, but millions of unsung homemakers worldwide do the same in their own homes.

Children aside, some wives resent "serving" their husbands. A few generations ago, a homemaker who felt she was serving her husband knew that he in turn was serving some greater goal (such as building a "good life" for her and their children). Today he may be serving nothing more than his ego. If so, why not serve her own and dump homemaking in favor of something higher-profile? In a Jewish marriage, however, both husband and wife serve only God.

More important, homemaking is not servitude. It's nurturing and kindness toward those we care most about.

When first married, I was sensitive to any overtones of "servitude." One evening, my husband was sitting at the dining room table studying while I was reading on the couch. Eventually, I noticed that he'd looked up, leaned back, and seemed a bit unsettled and distracted. He soon returned to his learning, but a

few minutes later he again stopped and looked restless. I asked if anything was wrong.

"I just feel like I need something... like maybe...
cookies," he said.

I raised my eyebrows. "Am I to understand that
because you're not getting up to get yourself some,
you'd like me to bring them to you?"

With the cutest, most endearing look he could
muster, he confessed, "Yeah."

I wasn't about to jump up. "One more question."
Knowing he was no male chauvinist (and also no
fool), I knew the answer, but I needed to hear it. "Do
you want me to bring you cookies because you think
I should wait on you, or because you want to feel nurtured?"

He didn't hesitate. "The second reason."

"In that case," I said, "I'd be happy to." I went into
the kitchen, arranged some homemade cookies on a
plate, poured a glass of milk, and brought them out
with my warmest smile. He thanked me and went
back to studying, happily munching away. That's not
servitude. It's love. (And a good husband will convey
the same to his wife.)

Nurturing brings us to yet another traditional
manifestation of womanhood. If home is where
one can receive love and affirmation, the activity
which can give these to a child is parenting—and
since women most often choose to be the primary
caretakers, this usually means mothering.

Mothering is powerful. In imbuing the next generation with Jewish values, the Jewish mother preserves
Judaism. But, you may counter, don't schools and

peers largely determine a child's interest in living Jewishly? That depends on the quality of mothering. If mothering means providing food and clothing, and ensuring the acquisition of social and academic skills, children will welcome other influences. But if mothering means, above all, lovingly instilling positive values—not only through teaching but, far more important, through modeling—a mother can have the strongest impact on her child.

This influence occurs on different levels. My parents tried to ensure that their values of secular education , culture, and comfort would dominate my life. At the same time, they—particularly my mother—unwittingly imparted far more significant convictions: that life is meaningful, that there's absolute morality, and that I should always believe in myself. These propelled me into a way of life that's quite different from theirs, but that has brought me tremendous happiness. My mother's unconscious influence was so powerful it undermined the very values she consciously sought to instill. (She's probably sorry she didn't give me what she wanted; I love her for giving me what she did.)

Yet this deeper, intangible kind of input appears to be waning. Back in 1988, *Dr. Spock on Parenting* lamented "the social ills and tragedies stemming from our spiritual poverty" and stated that "our society is disintegrating." In the same vein, Rebbetzin Tziporah Heller, a well-known educator, once commented, "In the '60s and '70s, people came to Judaism looking for spirituality. Today they come looking for morality." Much of the Western world sometimes seems like a shiny, waxed apple that's rotting at the core. The only solution is to reaffirm and strengthen internal influence upon children. And mothers are essential contributors.

Recognizing the value of mothering should lead you to ponder your future family life. If you and your spouse plan to work full-time, put your kids in daycare (or "self-care," as the latchkey option is now termed), and give them an hour or two of attention at the end of the day (if you have any energy left), please think twice. Children need quality time, but they also need *quantity* time. While a loving grandparent or long-term babysitter who shares your values can help, kids ultimately turn to Mom and Dad. And children don't learn the most important things in life, or enjoy sufficient parental closeness, via little blocks of concentrated attention, each of which "supposedly distills the essence of good parenting," in the words of Judith Wallerstein and Sandra Blakeslee (authors of *The Good Marriage*). "Children do not buy into the concept of quality time; they are foolish enough to clamor for 'time time'—bedtime, playtime, story time, soccer time, just-being-together time, and not-watching-the-clock time. They don't go for nouvelle-cuisine parenting no matter how prettily presented, for they have figured out that the helpings are too small and only leave them hungry for more." Children sense their need for an on-going parental presence, for they learn most through *osmosis*—from being around someone for hours each day from whom they can absorb what life is about.

Just as important, children must learn what *they* are about. A daycare professional told me, "The kids in my center are all socially well-adjusted and academically successful. But they don't know who they are. They have no real sense of self." Selfhood stems from a permanent place in the world and steady role models. Children also need love, and the best providers are those totally devoted to them and in love with their uniqueness—in other words, parents.

Yet internal influence comes first and foremost from women. A Jewish legal responsum written in the middle of the last century, by Rabbi Zalman Sorotzkin (of blessed memory), states that in times when faith must be strengthened, female education is our first priority, since women understand faith more readily than men and will influence their husbands and children (*Moznayim LeMishpat* 1:42). By nature and as wives and mothers, women hold the key to the future.

Mothering need not—and should not—be restricted only to one's own offspring. The first woman, Chava (Eve), was called "the mother of all living" even before bearing children (Genesis 3:20). Like helping, mothering extends far beyond any biological or adoptive relationship. By nurturing the best in others—including her husband, friends, friends' children, coworkers, students, acquaintances, and anyone she meets—any woman can provide some of the mothering the world so desperately needs.

Although people don't always appreciate the unseen and internal, God does. The story is told (*Baba Batra* 10b) of a Sage whose son nearly died and had a vision of the next world before returning to this one. When asked what he saw there, he said, "I saw a world upside-down. The upper was below and the lower was above."

His father replied, "You saw a clear world."

The world of truth is the opposite of this world. In the world to come, so much of what society esteems counts for nothing, while spirituality, nurturing, and all else we dismiss mean everything. The same will be true in the Messianic era, history's "next world."

Rabbi Aryeh Kaplan (of blessed memory) states that the feminine represents the future.* The role of women is to bring the values of the future into the present.

Change**

We've seen the importance of traditional feminine values. Yet upholding them was easier for our great-grandmothers than for many women today. Our world is still reeling from possibly the greatest social revolution in history: the women's movement, which has challenged gender roles within the family and in society.

The Torah world's reactions to feminism have often been either "for" or "against." Many left-wingers view it as a Godsend; many on the right view it as a threat. Yet feminism has clearly brought both positive and negative changes. In wading through the confusion, it helps to understand where the women's move-

---

* All citations of Rabbi Aryeh Kaplan are from his article "Male and Female," which appears in *Immortality, Resurrection, and the Age of the Universe: A Kabbalistic View* (New York: Ktav / AOJS, 1993).

** I credit a teacher of mine (affiliated with the Gerrer Chassidic community) with the ideas presented in this section ("Change"). For a full exposition, see "An Inner View of Feminism: The Secret of N'kevah T'sovev Gever," at www.orot.com.

ment may be coming from.

Understandings of gender have been shifting over the past few generations. Female intelligence has historically been conceived as concrete and this-worldly, suited primarily for earthbound realms such as home and hearth. Male intelligence, on the other hand, has been seen as more far-reaching and abstract, suggesting mental pursuits such as Torah study. Women therefore received their knowledge of abstract matters from men, who accordingly enjoyed greater social status.

I say *social* status because God sees things differently. According to *Seder HaDorot*, Rabbi Yehoshua, an outstanding Torah scholar, was told in a dream that his place in the next world would be with Nannas the Butcher. Astounded, he set out to discover who Nannas was, and after much searching, found him—a simple Jew extraordinarily devoted to his elderly parents. Upon seeing this, Rabbi Yehoshua exclaimed, "Fortunate am I that my lot is with Nannas the Butcher!" As a great Torah scholar, Rabbi Yehoshua occupied a much higher position in this world. Yet each man had realized his unique, God-given potential, and thus, in God's eyes, the two were equal. Similarly, despite their differences, men and women are equally capable of spiritual greatness in their own ways.

But women's "own way" isn't always what it used to be. An increasing number of women are mastering highly abstract thought, receiving doctorates in the sciences, mathematics, psychology, and philosophy. They have also reached new levels of Torah scholarship. In Judaism, nothing in history is incidental. In every generation, certain Divine energies shape our lives (Vilna Gaon, *Even Shelema* 11:9). Thus, if women are changing, the spiritual influences on our world are changing as well.

In fact, the changes we're seeing were predicted long ago, as a look at but a few of the many relevant Torah sources will show.

The Biblical Creation story recounts, "And God made the two great lights" (Genesis 1:16), implying that the sun and the moon were originally equal in size. But the verse continues, "the greater light to rule the day, and the smaller light to rule the night." The Talmud (*Chulin* 60b) tells us that the moon asked God, "Master of the World, can two kings share one crown?"—in other words, "Can two equally great lights coexist?" God replied, "Go then and diminish yourself." After trying unsuccessfully to console the moon, God acknowledged her pain, saying, "Bring an atonement for Me for making the moon smaller."

Traditionally, woman is represented by the moon and man by the sun. This midrash is telling us man and woman were created equally "luminous"—and light always represents Torah (see Proverbs 6:23). Woman initially penetrated the depths of Torah as did man. She then lost some of her abstract perception, and her path to spiritual perfection became more earthly.

In the future, however, women will regain their light, as Isaiah (30:26) prophecies: "The light of the moon shall be as the light of the sun." In the monthly sanctification of the new moon, we pray, "May it be Your will... to correct the flaw in the moon that there be no diminution in it. May the light of the moon be as the light of the sun and as the light of the seven days of Creation, as it was before it was diminished."

Jeremiah (31:21) is even more explicit about the coming changes in womankind: "God has created a new thing on earth, a female shall turn round [or encircle] a man." Rashi, the 11th-century Biblical commentator, understands from here that a woman will *court* a man (an interesting role reversal). He then offers an even more intriguing explanation: A female will turn round *to be*—turn *into*—a man. As Judaism wants men to be men and women to be women, what can this mean? Going back to the first century, *Targum Yonatan* provides an answer. Fascinatingly, this Aramaic translation renders the phrase "a woman shall turn round a man" as "the nation of the house of Israel will study Torah." Unlike the term *benei Yisrael*, which literally means "the sons of Israel," *beit Yisrael*, the *house* of Israel, refers to both males and females (as Rashi comments on Deuteronomy 34:8). In the future, women, like men, will involve themselves in Torah study.

More descriptive is the famous 19th-century Chassidic commentary *Ma'or VaShamesh* (on Exodus 15:20). Our world, *Ma'or VaShamesh* explains, is like a line. A line has a beginning and an end, with each point following the previous one and preceding the next. A line therefore symbolizes hierarchy. Likewise, in our world, Torah knowledge is hierarchical: Each of us knows more than one person, yet less than another, which means we each must turn to someone "ahead of" us for wisdom. In the future, however, the world will resemble a circle, with no beginning or end, no "ahead of" or "behind," only points equidistant from a center. According to *Ma'or VaShamesh*, "a female will *encircle* a man," with "female" representing humankind and "man" symbolizing God. (Though God transcends gender, God is a giver, and giving is traditionally described as "masculine," while receiving is "feminine.") Ultimately, all human souls will be like points on a circle, with God at the center. Rather than receiving knowledge from others, we will all learn directly from God, men and women alike. So states Jeremiah (31:33), "And they shall teach no more every man his neighbor..., for they shall all know Me, from the least of them to the greatest of them...."

These prophets and commentators are speaking of the redemption, the Messianic era. Yet as the redemption approaches, its changes start seeping into the world to prepare us (*Kuzari* 4:23). We are now generally believed to be nearing the redemption, and *these changes have begun*. Women are recognizing that they can develop themselves in ways they rarely were able to before. As Rabbi Aryeh Kaplan writes: "The new awareness among women is merely a glimpse of the light of the future Messianic Age."

Thus far, it may sound as if feminism is indeed a Godsend. Undoubtedly because of this reason, Rabbi Kaplan describes the positive phenomenon we're witnessing as "the new awareness among women," not "feminism" or "the women's movement."

Every energy that comes into the world can be used for holiness or misused for the opposite. For example, the Messianic era will also bring economic equality, tremendous scientific discovery, and the Jewish people's return to the Land of Israel, all of which have commenced. Yet the drive for economic equality fell partially into the wrong hands and became Soviet communism. Science, which can reveal God's greatness and benefit humankind, has also been a tool of atheism and mass destruction. And the return to Zion, miraculous as it is, has yet to culminate in a Torah-based society serving as a "light unto the nations."

So too with the change in women. Along with bringing much good, it has given rise to many unhealthy ideologies. While women now enjoy greater career opportunities and personal freedom, they are also victims of objectification, male expectations, and the devaluing of internality. As a result, while some females feel self-actualized and whole, many others are unhappy and torn (as documented, for instance, by Mary Pipher in *Reviving Ophelia*, and by Elizabeth Perle McKenna in *When Work Doesn't Work Anymore*). Perhaps Rabbi Kaplan was referring partly to this painful situation when he wrote: "The cataclysmic changes which take place as the end draws near will result in considerable dislocation, often referred to as the *chevlei Mashiach*, the birthpangs of the Messiah."

The Torah world as well has both gained and lost from the women's movement. In more liberal circles, which have welcomed feminism, females now benefit from the blessing of advanced Torah study and broader participation in Jewish life. Yet feminism's downside is not unknown there. In response, the more conservative-minded have taken great measures to defend and fortify the traditional female role. In so doing, however, some feel they have tended to reject any positive innovation that could be labeled feminist. Consequently, the Jewish community is precariously divided over women's issues.

Above all, feminism has left some Jews grappling with image and, more important, self-image. For once those outside Judaism championed female equality, they accused the "rabbinical establishment" of resisting it. This attack has created confusion, self-doubt, and a subtle erosion of Jewish pride within segments of the observant community.

Nonetheless, I believe we can embrace change in an authentically Jewish way: with unadulterated loyalty to both the letter and spirit of the Torah (as understood by the generation's leading rabbis) and to the feminine values crucial for our spiritual survival.

Bringing It Home

What does all this have to do with marriage preparation? Before committing to another person, you should contemplate these issues, because they'll decisively affect your lifestyle and happiness. I have definitely tried to influence your thinking in making the following points:

First, to dismiss traditional feminine values is to endanger ourselves spiritually. Though the moon will regain its light, it remains the moon, unalterably distinct from the sun. Females, as females, have a unique contribution to make, and the world depends on it. Internal consciousness is the soul of humankind, giving our children the strength and vision to be different and to make a difference.

Second, after affirming the feminine, every woman has the right to be who she is (as does every man). If you're a traditional female, know that you're following in the footsteps of generations of Jewish women who have shaped our destiny. If you're an abstract thinker, know that Jewish sources anticipate increasing numbers of women like you—no less or more valuable in God's eyes than their traditional counterparts, just different. Whoever you are, marry someone who appreciates you and wants you to grow into the best you possible.

Third, our response to feminism must be highly discriminating. Feminism is a very mixed bag—quite possibly because, as I have suggested, some of its potential sparks of holiness have been converted into destructive energy. We must sensitively select good from bad (with rabbinic advice), embracing what is holy and rejecting what is not.

Finally, true change requires patience. As I've said, this period in history has been called "the birthpangs of the Messiah," and we seem to be in the difficult, semifinal, "transition" stage of labor. At this point, birth is imminent, and the mother feels an overwhelming urge to push the baby out. But the urge is premature, so she must hold back. Today, because of the upsurge in women's equality, there is a great desire to push forward. Like a birth, however, change will fully emerge only when and how God wants it to.

Meanwhile, we must be who we are. We can encourage both women and men to affirm their individuality and express it in marriage. And in the Jewish world at large, we can promote healthy, gradual accommodation of women's new intellectual and spiritual needs, while strengthening all that has historically made Jewish women great. In this merit, may we hasten the revelation of that light on the horizon.

Part IV
Being Practical

After personal growth and an understanding of love and marriage, getting married requires practicality. You want to find the right person as efficiently and painlessly as possible. Chapter 6, "Leading with Your Head," explains Jewish dating and how to make it work for you. Chapter 7, "Steering Clear of Abuse," tells you how to avoid marrying an abusive personality and spot a potentially loving spouse.

Chapter Six
Leading with Your Head

D ating for marriage is complex. While God ultimately brings two people together, you must
invest effort in locating your soulmate. And
even if you "click" with someone (see Chapter 3), you
must decide logically if the match is right. Yet if you
leave things up to chance, your heart can push your
head out of the picture.

Jay had just finished his first year of medical school
and, he told me sorrowfully, ended a year-long relationship with Melissa.

"I grew up in an affluent community outside New
York where I basically had everything given to me.
But I've always been an idealist and very independent, and by the time I graduated high school, I knew I
didn't want my parents' materialistic lifestyle.
Instead, I decided to become a doctor and treat the
poor in a Third World country.

"Melissa's life," Jay continued, "was totally the
opposite. She's always had it tough and struggled for
everything she got. She's taken out a tremendous
amount of student loans and is working hard to put
herself through school. She's also very attached to her
family. Not only can't she afford to come with me to
Africa or Southeast Asia, she has no desire to. Her
dream is to find a job in a comfortable suburb not far
from her parents, pay off her debts, and contribute her
own way. Most of all, she wants to breathe easy for the
first time."

I was disturbed. "When did you find out about this problem?"

"Around our fourth date, when we started talking about what we each planned to do with our lives. But because we were already head over heels, we put it on the back burner. We figured that if we had something real, it would somehow work out.

"Over the next several months our relationship deepened. The 'issue' kept coming up, but each time we'd push it down. By the end of the year, we saw no solution. Our lives were headed in different directions. So we had to decide: Either spend the next three years together and say goodbye upon graduation, or say goodbye now. In the end, we broke up."

When Jay spoke again, his voice was full of pain. "We believed love would conquer all. I guess we were wrong."

"We Can Work It Out"?

One of the gravest dating mistakes is bonding emotionally with someone before knowing if you're fundamentally compatible. No matter how much you have going for yourselves as a couple, one major difference can leave you with no future together. Your partner may love his New York life; your dream is *aliya* (immigration to Israel). He wants a wife who'll work so he can pursue full-time, long-term Torah study; you want to stay home with your children while your husband provides the income. Some issues are irreconcilable, and the resulting break-ups are painful, putting you back at square one in finding a lasting relationship.

"But if two people love each other enough to want to get married, can't they compromise?" you may ask. Not always. You can't live simultaneously in New York and Israel; and unless he's quite wealthy, a man generally can't study Torah full-time without his wife's financial assistance. Even when serious compromises are made, they can leave a residue of unhappiness which eats away at a marriage. Rather than workable solutions, they may be desperate, after-the-fact attempts to preserve a relationship that never should have been.

Where *should* two people compromise? If you're both mature, you and your spouse should be able to work out whether to sleep with the window open or closed, where to vacation, and how to spend your money. But neither of you can compromise your fundamental beliefs and aspirations. *You can't give up who you are for another*. Nor should you want anyone to do so for you. For love isn't only loving the other's personality. As we said in Chapter 4, it's appreciating the other's goodness—which includes loving his principles and ambitions, loving her dreams and wanting her to realize them. If your values and goals are too different, you may love each other, but you may not be able to live together.

Of course, not compromising on who you are assumes you *are* someone, and you love *yourself*. I know a guy whose girlfriend broke up with him because he didn't share her spiritual ideals. Devastated, he promised he'd "do anything" to get her back, starting with dumping his values, aims, and lifestyle and adopting hers. She was overjoyed. I wasn't. Anybody willing to give up everything for somebody is a nobody, and being pursued by a nobody is nothing to cheer about. If you can imagine trading in your convictions for a relationship, or delighting that someone would do so for you, take stock. A person with self-esteem is a somebody and wants to marry one.

One often unresolvable issue (as mentioned at the end of Chapter 2) is religion. Sometimes a person newly "turned on" to Judaism, or a lapsed religious Jew intending to return, becomes involved with someone less observant, hoping he or she will "rise to the occasion." Yet wishful thinking doesn't create reality. And compromise may leave the more religious partner sad and lonely, and the less religious one resentful.

Years ago, I assisted in an educational program for Jewish adults. Among the participants were a newly observant young man and his long-time, non-observant girlfriend. She'd been grudgingly accommodating his growing religiosity, and he'd brought her to the seminar in the hope of inspiring her. But it wasn't happening, and things were going downhill fast. In the hotel lobby on Shabbat afternoon, I witnessed their breakup. In tears, the young woman headed for the exit, her purse on her shoulder.

"Wait!" her ex-boyfriend shouted after her. "If you leave this hotel carrying your purse, you'll be breaking Shabbat!"

She spun around to face him. "What does it matter anymore?"

I often wonder what would have happened had they compromised and married. I imagine her angrily reminding him at every marital dispute, "I'm doing this religious stuff only for you!" while he'd be equally bitter about how much more he could be doing without her. Embarking upon a marriage in which one or both of you have sacrificed something essential for the other is asking for trouble.

In short, love *doesn't* always conquer all. To build a future with someone, your relationship must not only *feel* right, but *be* right. Its foundation must be more than emotional. So why even date someone about whom you know little? Why not first find out whether your values and goals are compatible?

And thus we have what's known as the *shidduch* ("match") dating system.

You may have bad associations with the word *shidduch*. Perhaps you've seen *Fiddler on the Roof*, in which the doddering old matchmaker declares, "She's ugly and he's blind, so it's a perfect match!" Or there's the equally inept modern version: "He's 24, she's 22, they're both tall and American—let's set them up!"

Leaving parodies aside, let's talk about the real thing.

Intelligent Dating

Shidduch dating has four characteristics.

First, it assumes you're ready to get married. That means you're reasonably mature, know who you are, and have some idea of where you're heading and the kind of person you want. You also know what's negotiable and what isn't. This concept of being thought out, even to the point of having a mental "shopping list" of qualities you're seeking, may offend some. (Funny how rationalism in relationships bothers us, as if using your head means you have no heart.) If you're honest, though, you'll probably admit to a somewhat fuzzy "check list" in the back of your mind—and *shidduch* dating asks you to clarify it.

Second, a *shidduch* is arranged through a third party. He or she must understand you, be fairly wise and perceptive, and be able to introduce you to someone fundamentally compatible. (Excluded are well-meaning individuals whose eagerness to see you married overrides their ability to discern who's appropriate.) Your pool of potential "matchmakers" therefore may or may not include parents, siblings, friends, teachers, community members, rabbis, rabbis' wives, and others. After a date, your third party can also act as a go-between, relaying each person's impressions to the other, so neither need suffer face-to-face rejection before a relationship gets off the ground. This third party can troubleshoot as well. A man I know came back from a first date with a young woman who, to his exasperation, didn't stop talking the entire two hours. "She was probably nervous," the woman who set them up told him. "Try going out a couple more times." He did, and by the third date they were conversing normally. They're now happily married.

Third, both before and during dating, your "matchmaker" and other people you enlist gather insights into any prospective partner. In traditional circles, parents are especially active in collecting this information; if yours aren't, *you* should be. Those who have known your date longer or in different contexts can bring the picture into sharper focus, clarifying whether to pursue the relationship. (More about this ahead.)

Finally, *shidduch* dating includes no touching—being *shomer negiah*. While ridiculously difficult if you intend to hang out together for a few years, this self-control is definitely feasible in a shorter-term, marriage-directed relationship. Many insist, of course, that "trying things out" helps determine compatibility in marriage. All the evidence indicates they're dead wrong, for theirs is a pitifully shallow conception of sexuality. *True sexuality expresses not only who you are, but your feelings for your partner and the quality of your relationship.* Neither positive nor negative premarital experiences can predict the future, because without the love and emotional intimacy that come with marriage, your true sexual self can't come to the fore.

Strange as it may sound, *postponing* physical contact is actually the best way to assess compatibility. It promotes objectivity, letting you see the other without the illusions frequently created by physical closeness. It fosters a genuine, person-to-person (rather than body-to-body) connection. It helps you discover if you can appreciate the other not for how good he or she makes you feel but for who he or she actually is. Being *shomer negiah* is therefore essential in acquiring perspective on the big question: "Is this the person I want to spend the rest of my life with?" (All these points and more are discussed at length in my book *The Magic Touch*.)

Dating for marriage, using an intermediary, doing research, and being *shomer negiah* all help you put your head before your heart, and constitute "religious dating." Beyond that, dating is dating. You have to see if there's personal connection and physical attraction, if there can be mutual respect and admiration, if you can laugh together and deal with each other's weaknesses. And therefore you have to be honest and real.

I vividly remember my first *shidduch*. I was terrified. What should I wear, how should I act, what should I say? Suddenly, from some earlier memory, I heard my mother's soothing voice: "Just be yourself."

The first and last rule of religious dating is *be yourself*. Don't pretend to be anything you aren't (no matter how much you wish you were), or talk yourself into wanting something other than what you genuinely need. A nature-loving friend of mine used to tell her "third parties" only that she wanted to marry a serious student of Torah. Finally, realizing she wasn't being completely honest, she began requesting a *"frum* [religious] mountain man." Soon after, she married someone who, in addition to studying and teaching Torah, loves the outdoors, and hiking is one of their favorite pastimes.

If you've become observant in adulthood, remember that while your beliefs, practices, aspirations, and even character may have changed, your essential nature hasn't. You may be more spiritually developed, but you're still you—and that means you need someone fundamentally similar to whom you would have married before becoming religious.

After meeting Avraham, the man I later married, my mother was relieved. "I know both your lives are very different from what they were," she told me, "and much of your connection is based on common spiritual aspirations. But even if you weren't religious, I could totally see you together." She was right—and that's largely why our marriage works.

So be true to yourself in dating. Present yourself as

who you are. And while being open to advice, trust your gut feelings (which God gave you for a reason) in deciding who's right for you.

Doing It Right

Even if your third party ensures that anyone you go out with is "in the ballpark," how can you get the most out of dating? Let me offer some practical suggestions.

First, find someone who can advise you (preferably free of charge).* Your third party can often fill this role, or you may prefer an outsider. In addition to understanding how to maximize religious dating, your advisor must appreciate your personality and needs. I once told a woman that I intended to stop seeing someone because I didn't feel he and I could converse intellectually. She shook her head. "You're making a mistake," she stated emphatically. "You'll be busy all day with the house and kids while he's out working or learning. How much time do you think you'll have to talk philosophy?" I winced. She's definitely telling me something about *her* marriage, I thought, but not about the kind I need. Anyone offering guidance must respect who you are.

Start the dating process by informing anyone and everyone that you're ready for marriage, even if some of them know the same singles. While one person (whom I highly respect) told me she would have never set me up with Avraham because we seemed so different, another sensed our deeper affinity. Never

---

*To speak to a trained dating (and engagement) advisor, e-mail advisor@sassonvsimcha.org.

rely on just one third party.

On the first few dates, don't discuss anything too serious (although "too serious" will depend on how intense you both are). You already know the two of you have much in common—just get to know each other. Relax, converse, and try to banish expectations (such as "fireworks") or superficial appraisals ("He/she seems too this, not enough that..."). Show that you're happy to meet him or her and anticipate a nice time, regardless of where it leads. Don't interview your date. Take a genuine interest in his or her life. Listen. Don't give her reason to complain, "He seemed nice, but all he did was talk about himself." Most of all, *be warm*. Make him feel good with appropriate compliments ("It must have taken a lot of work to achieve what you have"). This appreciation will open you *both* up to positive feelings. And start seeing if you two can develop the mutual respect and admiration that define a healthy relationship.

Keep these initial dates short (no longer than two hours) and no more frequent than twice a week. Seeing someone new can unleash an onslaught of emotions. Taking it slow gives you time to process.

The following story illustrates how crucial emotional space can be. Tamar had a wonderful first date with an attractive, charming man who displayed great interest in her. Because he'd be in the country only two weeks, he asked to see her every evening, and she readily agreed. After 12 consecutive meetings, she was certain he was "it." The following night, however, they couldn't meet, and during that short break, Tamar suddenly realized she had some questions about this fellow. Their next date was on the eve of his departure, and he romantically proposed. Taken aback, Tamar stuttered that she wasn't ready to decide. He blew up. "I've spent a whole two weeks with you, and this is all you have to say!" he yelled. "Who do you think you are? You're not going to get away with this!" Tamar was shocked—and realized how close she'd come to a disastrous mistake. (See the next chapter, which deals with abusive personalities.)

If after the first and second dates, you could go either way, go out again. By the end of the third or fourth date, you should feel more; if not, this person probably isn't for you. If you're interested but he or she isn't, try not to take it personally (unless your third party can point to anything you need to work on). We all have our (usually subjective) reasons for being attracted to one person and not another. Trust that the right person is out there.

What should you look for when dating?

In a word, *quality*—and that's not external, but *internal*. Good looks, charm, and accomplishment can dazzle, but they can't replace such basics as character and spiritual aspirations. *You want to marry an essence, not an image.*

Efrayim was handsome, bright, successful, and charismatic, and had been a top student in his yeshiva. When he proposed, Rina felt like the luckiest woman in the world. After two years of marriage, she no longer did. Her husband had proven self-centered, not very giving, and unwilling to improve, insisting that she accept him as he was. Rina's close friend Toby learned a big lesson from this couple. She married a man who was, in her words, "nice-looking enough," had a smaller income but a big heart, and wanted to grow and make her happy—and 10 years later, she *still* feels lucky. (The qualities you should seek in a partner are the same ones *you* should have before marrying—see back in Chapter 2.)

In addition to essence, look for common sense. Married life is lived not in heaven but on earth. No matter what a wonderful *neshama* your spouse has, he or she must be able to negotiate the practical realities of this world, be it making a living, running a household, or some of each.

What similarities and differences should you seek? Your partner's nature should complement your own in some ways, but no rules can tell you how. One introverted intellectual may need someone equally quiet but more emotional; another may need someone equally brainy but more outgoing. You may want your opposite, but the differences between you must work. For example, if you're a slob who aspires to tidiness, you may be delighted with a neat freak, but he or she will probably find you intolerable—and you may find yourself yearning for the relaxed comfort of a fellow mess-maker. Bottom line: Look for someone you can live with and who can live with you.

Beyond clearly beneficial differences, *go for as many similarities as possible*. The more you have in common, the less you'll disagree, and the easier your relationship will be. Similar cultural, intellectual, and socioeconomic backgrounds are especially important, as these shape your marital expectations and your approach to issues such as child rearing and standard of living. Don't be concerned that you'll lack opportunities to grow through overcoming differences. *That one of you is male and the other female is difference enough.* Beyond that, God will give you the challenges you'll need.

The two of you must share the same religious aspirations. You needn't be in the same place, but you must be moving in the same direction (as illustrated earlier in this chapter and at the end of Chapter 2).

Physical attraction is important, but not immediately. I know couples who are now happily married because of one partner's willingness to see if the other would "grow on" him or her. So don't quickly reject anyone based on appearance unless he or she actually repulses you. Ask yourself: Are there times when you're more attracted to this person? Why? Can he or she do something about it? Don't measure your date against some preconceived "type"—try to view him or her without prejudice. You may come to appreciate her kind of beauty or how his personality colors his looks. Keep in mind that your spouse may bear no resemblance to the person you've imagined. As long as you see progress from date to date, stick it out.

Personal and emotional attraction can also take time. At this stage, neither of you is necessarily showing your true self. Don't assume you'll never feel what you need to just because you don't yet.

Three-quarters of an hour into their first date, Yaakov offered to walk Aviva home. "Listen," he told her, "I want to be straight with you. You're not for me."

Aviva felt no interest in him either, but she was ticked off and decided to let him have it. "I don't care if we go out again or not," she informed him icily, "but to think you know me after 45 minutes is ridiculously shallow."

An hour-long conversation ensued, which impressed each one with the other's willingness to communicate directly and honestly—and they went out again. Today they have an excellent marriage.

Likewise, don't write off a person for doing something stupid. Many young women have asked me, "How should I react to the fact that, at 11:30 at night, my date said goodbye and left me alone at a bus stop?" My answer: The first time, chalk it up to ignorance. But if you go out again, bring it up. A sincere apology from him and a change in his conduct will say more about his character than his mistake does.

All in all, *give it a chance.*

After meeting a few times, if you sense a relationship is developing, lengthen your dates. However, see each other only two or three times a week for another couple of weeks. Talk briefly on the phone in between. Taking it slowly may be hard, but you don't want to risk emotional inundation and confusion (more common among females). As things become more serious, you may need to see how it feels to be together more, or you may still need space.

What should you do on these expanded dates? Since dating is somewhat artificial, make it more natural and "real." Spend time together in different places, doing different things, and in the company of different people. Include many informal and fun activities that encourage you each to relax and be yourselves. Avoid overly "romantic" environments— you want to remain as objective as possible. Pay attention to subtle reflections of personality, such as how he drives and parks. Observe how she relates to others. If the opportunity arises, see how he behaves on Purim(!). Note how she reacts to frustrations, like missing a bus or finding no empty tables at a restaurant. (One couple I know were caught in a downpour, and the woman's easy-going, playful reaction to getting drenched propelled her date towards deciding she was the one.) Watch how she deals with disagreements. Can he air his opinions, respect yours, and work maturely to resolve conflicts? Can she take criticism? Can he forgo having the last word? See what makes her happy, sad, excited, or upset. Introduce him to people you know and ask their impressions. Meet his friends as well—the company one keeps says a lot.

So do role models. When my friend Marisa met her husband-to-be's rabbi—a family man who loved Torah, people, and life—she knew she'd chosen the right person. On the other hand, you may discover the opposite. I once dated a very nice guy who seemed more conservative than I. We decided to spend Shabbat together. For dinner, he brought me to his favorite rabbi, who sat and led the conversation while his wife served and cleared. I was uncomfortable. For lunch, I brought him to a home I liked, where both husband and wife discussed Torah at the table and cleaned up together. He was uncomfortable. And that clinched it.

Again, gender roles merit consideration. There's beauty and wisdom in the traditional ones, but no less in your unique personality and needs (see back in Chapter 5). You also have conscious and unconscious feelings about "what a wife should do" and "what a husband should do," stemming from what *your* parents did and whether you liked it—and these feelings come out once you marry.

Progressive-minded, Ashkenazic Donna married a man from a traditional Sephardic home who nevertheless professed great flexibility about gender roles. Yet once married, he discovered that in order to feel nurtured, he needed his wife to treat him much as his mother had treated both him and his father. Unfortunately, what was natural and comfortable to him felt oppressive to her—and they realized they had a big problem. Beware of someone with a background very different from yours, unless he or she produces evidence (not just words) of compatibility. (Interestingly, Arlie Hochschild reports in *The Second Shift* that the husbands most likely to help at home were not those whose fathers had done so or who had themselves been trained to lend a hand, but those whose fathers had been detached or absent and whom they consequently vowed *not* to be like.)

I was the one to bring up marital roles when Avraham and I were dating. "I don't have a black-and-white approach to who does what in the home," I told him. "I also don't need to split it 50-50. I'm kind of a 70-30 type. How do you feel?"

"I can't see myself doing cooking and laundry," he said (since his mother had always done them). "But I don't mind pitching in with shopping, cleaning, and other things."

I disliked shopping and hated cleaning, but I didn't mind laundry and actually enjoyed cooking. It sounded like this could work.

"Full-length" dates are also the place to start discussing values, beliefs, and goals in detail. You know the large puzzle pieces fit—now see if the smaller ones can as well.

As you move into more intellectual territory, continue building emotional intimacy. Reveal more about yourself and your past, and ask your date to do the same. (Ask your rabbi what negative information to disclose.) Share more about how you became who you are. See if you can each be vulnerable, and if your companion responds with warmth and caring. When a woman I know lost her grandfather, her date's empathy and compassion showed her she could count on him emotionally.

Learn about the other's background, family life, and activities, weaving these topics into the conversation rather than resorting to interrogation. What has been his education? What jobs has she held? What kinds of friendships and, if relevant, romances (without details) has he had? Asking such questions may sometimes be uncomfortable, but it's reasonable if you're getting serious. If it feels inappropriate, you haven't dated long enough.

A friend dated someone who, after several weeks, still couldn't share with her. She decided to ask about his past relationships with women, and found out they'd always been brief and superficial. A counselor helped her see he had a serious problem with emotional intimacy, and she decided to stop seeing him. A man who similarly wondered why his date couldn't open up learned she'd lost her father and suffered a broken engagement. Realizing she wasn't yet ready to make herself vulnerable, he gave her the extra time she needed. Knowing the past can illuminate the present.

Once you feel "this could be it" (or preferably even earlier), make sure to meet and spend time with each other's families. (I know traveling may be expensive, but it's worth it.) We absorb the behaviors we've been raised with, both positive and negative, so unless we labor to change, we become strikingly like our parents. (After each visit with her mother, my friend's husband jokes, "I forgive you.") These similarities will be especially prominent once we ourselves marry and have children. So notice: How do his parents relate to each other and to him and his siblings? How does the family as a whole interact? While things may have changed since her childhood, the basic dynamics (sensitivity, communication, expression of affection, or the opposites) are probably the same and will undoubtedly shed light on the kind of spouse (and parent) she is likely to be.

I know a couple whose dating relationship was progressing, but the man was bothered by something he couldn't define. Then he met the woman's highly critical mother and suddenly understood that his date showed signs of the same disposition. My friend Tehilla had the opposite experience. After dating Rafael for several weeks, she met his father and older brothers—three exceptionally sensitive, spiritual, emotionally tuned-in males. From the beginning she'd sensed that this quiet guy had a heart of gold, but seeing the men with whom he'd grown up and the warmth of their interactions confirmed it. Families can tell you a great deal.

As often as possible, step back from your relationship and do a reality check. Among other things, make sure you're aware of at least some of the other person's flaws. No one, no matter how wonderful, is perfect. If you think otherwise, you may be idealizing—keep going out until your picture is more realistic. On the other hand, your date may be afraid of revealing his true self, in which case you must learn why. If you've picked up on any hints of physical or mental illness, investigate them. If you don't discover anything, but something still feels "off," go with your intuitions.

A young woman I know was dating a man who seemed considerate and caring yet closed, leading to uneasy silences. The person who set them up urged her to overlook this trait, attributing it to the strict yeshiva environment in which he was raised, which left him unaccustomed to speaking with women. Against her instincts, they married—and he turned out to be severely disturbed and abusive. Ideally, you should feel whole about whom you've chosen to marry. If you don't, you may need professional advice about whether to proceed. In the end, though, the decision is yours.

Some problems, rather than being objective grounds for terminating a relationship, depend upon your reaction. After a few dates, Chana informed Shmuel that she was diabetic, assuring him she'd been taking care of herself for years. Having lost a brother to hypoglycemia, however, Shmuel couldn't handle Chana's illness. The next man she dated had no such anxiety. Whenever issues arise, seek advice, but go with your own feelings.

Every step of the way, turn to others who know the person you're dating—roommates, neighbors, rabbis, teachers, students, employers, employees, coworkers, *anyone*—and ask their input. (In so doing, both sides must avoid *lashon hara*. A book like *Chofetz Chaim: A Lesson a Day* by Rabbi Shimon Finkelman and Rabbi Yitzchak Berkowitz explains what information is forbidden, permissible, or obligatory to give.) Rather than an open-ended inquiry ("What can you tell me about [the person you're dating]?"), pose specific questions requiring specific answers.

Doing your homework can spare you the heartache of dissolving a serious relationship, engagement, or even marriage. I know of a woman who wed a man without knowing he was an international gangster. More common are stories like that of the young man whose in-laws had concealed their daughter's emotional instability (naively believing that once she married, everything would be fine). According to a rabbi who works in rabbinical courts, the majority of cases in which a husband refuses to divorce his wife can be avoided via thorough premarital checking. While your date is probably normal and healthy, you can't assume it. Researching a prospective marriage partner is not some old-fashioned idea. It's a *must*.

If (after talking it over with others) you decide this person isn't right for you, don't be afraid to end the relationship. Anything that bothers you now will probably bother you even more once you're married. "Better" a broken relationship or even engagement than a divorce.

If you find yourself thinking in terms of "we," however, you're close to deciding "yes." At this point, you may profit from some standard premarital couples' counseling with a qualified, religious professional. You'll gain invaluable insight into yourself, your partner, and your relationship, and learn communication skills that will help once you're married. (And once you're engaged, find out if there's a Jewish marriage preparation course you can take.)

Even dating as I've described it will not eliminate post-wedding surprises. But they'll be ones you can deal with. The purpose of religious dating is to reach the point of knowing, "This is the person with whom I want to, and can, make a relationship work."

How long should it take to decide? As you've probably realized, dating is more complicated than it once was. When people lived in small, homogeneous communities in which everyone knew everybody else, values and beliefs were predictable, and character references more attainable. With the transience of modern life and the diverse influences on our thinking and behavior, your date is far less known to the third party, no matter how much research he or she may have done. At the same time, our subjective expectations of marriage are much higher (for better or worse). You must therefore find out more for yourself—and this means dating longer. I can't tell you how long, because what's important is not the quantity but the *quality* of your time together. You're ready to make a decision not after some magic number of weeks, months, or dates, but when you've learned what's necessary about the other. You may feel you "know" earlier, but keep going out until you *really* know.

Some people disagree with the need to date this long, because "you never really know a person until you're married." Absolutely true, but you'll certainly know more and be more likely to make the right decision after dating as outlined above than after a handful of meetings in your best dress and on your best behavior.

Others point out that "the right match is all *siyata diShmaya* [help from Heaven] anyway." Yes, God provides your soulmate—so pray to recognize him or her—but God still expects us to act responsibly and intelligently, as in every other area of life.

Others actually object to prolonged dating, worrying that the couple will stop being *shomer negiah*. This is a real concern. So keep to well-lit, public places, tie your hands behind your back, join a *shomer negiah* support group—whatever works for you. If tension enters the relationship, realize its source and, if necessary, take a short break. But don't let fear of temptation—or anything else—stampede you into a premature decision.

A Match Made in Heaven

Of course, dating must end. This is where some people get stuck. "Commitment-phobia" is widespread these days (as mentioned in Chapter 1), particularly among the increasing number who've suffered traumas such as abandonment or divorce. On the other hand, cold feet may signal something wrong in the relationship. A qualified counselor can help you understand what's going on, and if you conclude that the relationship is right, help you work past your fears. (If anxiety arises after you're engaged, don't set a date until it's resolved.)

Often, however, people are reluctant to commit simply because doing so closes off other options. After all, how do you know there isn't someone better?

A friend of mine has the best answer. "You don't," she says. "Somewhere out there is a man who's a better match for me than my husband. Probably even several. And they should all be as happy with their soulmates as I am with mine." God brings a certain person and not others into your life for reasons only God knows. If you choose wisely, he or she *becomes* your soulmate.

One of the seven blessings recited under the *chupa* (wedding canopy) reads: "Gladden the beloved companions as You gladdened Your creature in the Garden of Eden from aforetime." Since Chava was the only woman on earth, Adam could rejoice in knowing they were meant for each other. For the rest of us, marriage requires a leap of faith. But if you use your head and heart—in that order—you too will be as sure as humanly possible that you've found your soulmate.

Chapter Seven
Steering Clear of Abuse

Sadly, spousal abuse has become a concern in the Jewish world. Though uncommon in marriages built on Jewish values, it exists, and communities are addressing it.

Singles can and must learn to recognize a potential abuser before marrying him or her. On the one hand, if this training isn't hard-hitting, it won't be effective. You can't fight tetanus without a vaccine, and you can't escape the risk of abuse (which is likelier, Rabbi Abraham Twerski points out, than stepping on a rusty nail) without equally strong preventive medicine. On the other hand, I don't want to scare anyone away from marriage altogether. So I'll attempt to strike a balance and create a healthy level of awareness.

A person suffering from deep-seated feelings of inferiority and self-hatred acquired in childhood may attempt to boost his self-esteem by asserting power over others. This can express itself as physical or emotional abuse. While abusive personalities exist in both sexes, they're more common among males, who are usually stronger physically and economically, and have a greater inborn desire to "lead." Consequently, and because of the awkwardness of repeatedly writing "he or she," "his or her," etc., I'll refer to the abuser in the masculine, without intending to exclude female abusers.

It's important to differentiate between a basically

normal person who sometimes behaves abusively, and someone with a personality disorder. Someone who occasionally "loses it" and is abusive has a major character defect, but he can look at himself objectively, feel genuine remorse, and want to change. Therapy may help, depending on the depth of his childhood wounds and his resolve. Unfortunately, his problem may be detected only after the *chupa*, when triggered by marriage-related stress such as finances or children.

An abusive personality disorder is far more serious, yet also more recognizable, and it's therefore what I'll be discussing. This person's wounds are so deep and pervasive that relating abusively feels normal to him. He's typically blind to his illness and refuses help. Fortunately, he can almost always be seen for what he is before marriage, *provided you date him long enough and pay close attention to your relationship*. I know several women, from secular to strictly observant, whose husbands turned out to be abusers, and in every case, the warning signals were there before marriage. These women (and their friends) just didn't recognize them—or ignored them.

Red Lights

How can you identify a potential abuser while you're dating?

The best way is to familiarize yourself with abusive personality traits. While few abusers will possess every one, all will possess some. The following list describes what each trait looks like in marriage, how it may manifest itself in dating, and how normal people behave instead. The more said, the scarier it all sounds, but *don't overreact*. Don't excuse yourself midway through a date to consult this list anxiously in the restroom. Don't deliberately spill hot soup on your date's lap to test his reaction to stress. Go out ready to believe he's the fine, decent human being he's overwhelmingly likely to be. Also realize that *most normal people* (including me, and probably you) *have some of these characteristics*, albeit in milder form. If insensitivity, criticality, or intolerance always spelled abuse, most peoples' kids would be taken away, and marriages would be over before they began. However, if someone demonstrates not one or two of these behaviors but *several*, and not once or twice but *repeatedly*, a red light should go on.

Here are the traits:

1) **He is very controlling and possessive.** This is the primary characteristic of an abusive personality, and it's discussed at greater length ahead.

> *In marriage:* He'll control every detail and moment of your life—your dress, finances, social life, religious observance, and more—to the point of making you his puppet.

> *While dating:* He may keep tabs on where you go, how you spend your money, and how much time you spend with whom. He may attempt to influence your behavior and thinking. He may want you available to him constantly. He may push the relationship forward rather than letting it progress naturally.

>> Whenever Yehuda called Miriam's cell phone (as he did several times a day) and heard noise on her

end, he'd quickly ask, "Where are you? Who's that? What's going on?" If Marci quoted someone's opinion, Avi insisted that she disregard it. Jerry always decided where he and Rhonda went. Evan resented that Dana wouldn't agree to marriage until he'd met her parents, and after the meeting, he insisted they get engaged right away.

The normal people you date will want to spend time with you but won't demand it. Though interested in your life, they'll respect your privacy. If you're uncertain about the relationship, they may try and sway you but without heavy pressure. They'll know where they end and you begin, and recognize you as a person in your own right.

2) **He has a Jekyll/Hyde (two-sided) personality.**

In marriage: He'll display respectability, charm, and charisma, alternating with dark, mean, monstrous behavior.

While dating: In the beginning, you may see only his good side. (I've heard abusive fiancés described as "very suave.") Most of his goodness, however, is "too good to be true." You may eventually start seeing through his image.

Steve was a perfect gentleman with Erin, but cold and hard with others for no apparent reason. When she asked for an explanation, he would brush her off, saying, "It's not worth talking about."

The normal people you date will be good *and* true. They may occasionally misbehave but will acknowledge it. Their moods will mesh within a pleasant and consistent personality.

3) **He is power-hungry and manipulative.**

In marriage: He'll depersonalize you into an object to exploit, use religion to dominate you, and seek revenge against anyone (including you) he feels has wronged him.

While dating: He may display great interest in how much money you or your parents have and in using your resources for his own ends. He may buy you expensive gifts to win you over or get something from you. He may order others around and make macho pronouncements like "I'm the boss around here." He may do all he can to get his way.

> Although Josh knew Amy was *shomer negiah*, he kept pressuring her to get physical. When Penny told Nathan she needed her car back earlier than he thought was necessary, he deliberately returned it late. When another driver cut Avner off, Avner did the same to him, then drove very slowly while grinning into the rearview mirror. When Julie wanted to break up with Phil, he threatened to badmouth her.

The normal people you date will be interested in who you are, not what you have or can do for them, and they won't want to "rule" you.

4) **He can't empathize.**

In marriage: He'll be oblivious to your needs and feelings, and to how his behavior affects you. He'll be unable to relate intimately consistently.

While dating: He may be overly solicitous to cover for all he's lacking inside. He may claim his hurtful remark was only in jest. He may be indifferent, inconsiderate, and/or disrespectful. He may withdraw when upset. He may be cruel to animals.

> Alex laughed in a strange, excited way when Sharon recounted someone's "humorous" misfortune, and upon hearing other bad news, he would either ignore it or shrug and say, "Life goes on," or "He must have deserved it." Beth one day noticed Eric across the street, kicking a passing cat.

The normal people you date may sometimes lack sensitivity but will feel for others, treating them as they treat you. If they hurt your feelings, you'll sense it was due to ignorance, not meanness, and they'll be genuinely sorry.

5) **He defies limits.**

In marriage: He always sees how far he can push.

While dating: He may try to get away with whatever he can in all kinds of small (or even large) ways, including breaking the law.

> When Yossi saw a half-empty ice cream container in Shani's aunt's refrigerator, he suggested they finish it without her knowing. Joe wanted to show Michelle the view from a non-public place and, upon finding the door locked, plotted how they could break in without alerting the security guard.

The normal people you date may be tempted by minor transgressions but will essentially obey the law and respect rules.

6) **He is compulsive and makes unrealistic demands.**

In marriage: He'll be petty and have unreasonable expectations, becoming furious when things don't go as they "should" and making you feel guilty and ashamed when you don't meet his standards.

While dating: He may obsess over what's external, criticizing your appearance or fixating on some detail of religious observance that he wants you to correct. He may overreact negatively to anything unexpected.

> When Elisheva suggested a change in venue for their date, Bob got very upset. When Rivky showed up in a skirt Mordechai thought was too short, he was nasty and cold the whole evening. Ari shamed Stacey for not making a *frum* enough impression, insisting she incorporate more Yiddish and "yeshivish" into her speech.

The normal people you date may be critical but will tolerate imperfections, including yours. They'll appreciate your looks but focus on deeper aspects of you.

7) **He is arrogant, self-centered, and intolerant.**

In marriage: He'll view everything from his own perspective, hold himself above almost everyone else, and be heavily prejudiced against people from different religious or cultural backgrounds. He'll exhibit rigid gender-stereotyping and contempt for women.

While dating: He may enjoy deriding or belittling others. He may react poorly to losing an argument. He may lack mentors, refuse help, and object to consulting an authority (such as a rabbi) about anything important or personal.

> Larry denigrated Shoshana's less religious relatives despite striking gaps in his own observance, and ridiculed rabbis who opposed his views. Hal often told his mother to be quiet. Tzvi made fun of Susan for going to "lower level" Torah classes. When Esther mentioned she wanted a master's degree, Adam responded, "So you're going to be

one of those big-shot career women?"

The normal people you date may be judgmental and even occasionally arrogant or disdainful. Yet you'll see humility as well: They'll look up to wiser individuals and seek their input and regard others' opinions. They'll respect their parents. While they may deride others' beliefs or lifestyles, they won't ridicule fellow human beings. They'll be generally open, not closed, to others.

8) **He externalizes problems.**

In marriage: He'll blame everyone (especially you) for his conduct and anything that happens to him, and will justify cruelty by saying you deserved it.

While dating: He may refuse to accept rebuke and hold others responsible for his problems or behavior. (Note: You are *never* responsible for another adult's behavior.)

> Dov blamed his bounced check on the new bank manager. Gary told Adrienne, "It's your fault I get so angry."

The normal people you date may be defensive but will eventually look at themselves honestly, admit they're wrong, and take responsibility for their actions.

9) **He is paranoid.**

In marriage: He'll falsely accuse you, fear others are taking advantage of him or going behind his back, and see himself as a victim.

While dating: He may take innocent mistakes personally, or jump on anyone he feels has "attacked" him or may yet do so.

> When a child accidentally ran into Levi, he shoved the boy off and yelled at him. When Brad saw Joanne looking in the direction of another guy, he accused her of being interested in him. When Avigayil showed up five minutes late for a date, Shlomo told her angrily, "You know I hate waiting for you—you did that on purpose to upset me."

The normal people you date may occasionally wonder if someone has something against them but will dismiss unwarranted concerns and generally appraise reality accurately.

10) **He lies, deceives, minimizes, and denies.**

In marriage: He'll scheme to get out of what he gets himself into.

While dating: He may make excuses, including outright lies, for not being where or doing what he was supposed to; wriggle out of deceptions he's been caught in; and dismiss his misconduct as unimportant or as if it never happened. He may claim to have achieved things he hasn't.

> Chayim told Yehudit he'd been at yeshiva all day when in fact he'd gone downtown with friends. Aaron told Dina he was pursing his M.A., whereas he was still negotiating his B.A. despite being a few credits short.

The normal people you date may try to excuse behavior they're ashamed of but will essentially be honest.

11) **He can't deal with anger, frustration, or stress.**

In marriage: He'll be unusually nervous and hot-tempered, cope poorly, explode easily, and react physically (e.g., throwing or breaking things).

While dating: His anger may "leak out" in great impatience, overreactions to everyday aggravations (like traffic jams, spills, and tardiness), or even small outbursts.

> Jeff blew up when a waiter forgot to bring water. When Andrea made Paul mad, he stopped the car, slammed the keys down on the dashboard, and stormed off. Whenever Ilana pointed out that he'd done something wrong, Roy started breathing quickly and looked as if he might lose control.

The normal people you date will be impatient within normal bounds and lose their temper only occasionally and moderately, if at all. Stress won't overwhelm them.

12) He is physically and/or verbally aggressive.

In marriage: He'll bully others physically and / or by name-calling and ridicule, and use force to get what he wants.

While dating: He may be rude and combative toward others, drive extremely aggressively and competitively, call other drivers and pedestrians names, treat others roughly, and use force against inanimate objects.

> When Jeremy was politely told that the table he'd sat down at was reserved, he cursed the waiter under his breath. When no Coke came out of the vending machine, Kurt kicked it angrily. Bob looked for opportunities to smash his opponents during hockey games.

The normal people you date may become contentious when provoked but not often. They'll play sports for fun, not for violence.

13) **He is self-deprecating and tends toward depression.**

In marriage: He'll say he hates himself and feels like killing himself, or even threaten suicide. (This self-loathing in no way contradicts an abuser's arrogance, which merely masks his deep feelings of inferiority.)

While dating: He may put himself down, appear pathetic (often also for manipulative purposes), or make strong statements about what he'll do if you don't marry him.

> If a day went by in which Yitzchak didn't see Mindy, he'd tell her he was depressed. When Yael doubted their future together, Ben told her, "It's my fault; nothing good has ever happened to me," and when she broke up with him, he despaired, "I'm going to seclude myself and never come out."

The normal people you date will display healthy self-esteem. Even a major set-back won't destroy them, and they'll recover in a reasonable amount of time.

14) **He has a history of violence, even if channeled acceptably.**

In marriage: You'll discover that he was a bully when younger, and/or that his work provides an outlet for abusive behavior.

While dating: He may have undesirable friends or a job a kind, sensitive person wouldn't want.

> Todd told Ellen he'd hung out with a rough crowd in high school. Stu had twice been arrested for punching someone. Eitan worked with the secret service interrogating suspected terrorists.

The normal people you date won't be violent. If their

job occasionally entails toughness (as with some policemen), they'll relate to it as an unfortunate necessity, not with pleasure.

15) **He has a history of substance abuse.**

In marriage: He'll do (or you'll discover he's done) a lot of drinking and/or drug taking.

While dating: He may mention how "wild and crazy" he is (or was) with friends and dismiss suggestions of dependency with statements like "We were just having fun."

> At weddings, Ilan would drink beyond all socially accepted norms, then brush off Lori's concerns with "Don't drive me crazy."

The normal people you date may have occasionally indulged in alcohol or drugs, but should have outgrown it and now drink sparingly. Any addictions should be demonstrably behind them (e.g., successful participation in Alcoholics Anonymous).

16) **He witnessed or suffered parental abuse, deprivation, or neglect.**

In marriage: You'll learn that one of his parents abused the other, or that one or both abused him. (Neglect and deprivation may constitute passive abuse.)

While dating: He may volunteer information about his childhood, but more likely you'll have to ask. If he's somewhat open, he may admit to resenting his parents; if he's closed, he may pretend they're perfect and not want you to meet them. If the truth is exposed and you express concern, he may protest that he would never repeat his parents' behavior and doesn't need professional help.

> Mark told Stephanie he'd been a latchkey kid and didn't get along with his largely absentee mother. Ken didn't tell Ronit his parents were separated and he had no contact with his violent father. When Eli mentioned there'd been physical abuse in his home and Karen asked if he thought he might act similarly with his own children, he responded angrily, "Shut up."

The normal people you date will come from, at the very least, non-dysfunctional homes. If not, they'll have undergone therapy and be willing to discuss their backgrounds and how they've worked through their problems.

It bears stressing: *No one of the above traits indicates an abusive personality.* Just as in a connect-the-dots picture, you must "connect" several characteristics for an abusive picture to emerge. Doing so requires stepping back and looking as objectively at possible at the other person and your interactions with him.

Once a relationship is off the ground, *control* (the first trait described) will become especially prominent and can be the key in identifying a potential abuser. The stumbling block is that *an abuser's control tactics can be wonderfully flattering.* Indeed, if you're wondering, "Why would anyone want to marry someone with any of these traits?" *this is why.* He may insist that you remain available via cell phone, saying he misses you so much. He may dictate your clothes and hairstyle, saying he loves looking at you. He may attempt to limit your interactions with others, saying he wants to spend all his time with you. He may be jealous if he sees you speaking to another male and push you to get engaged before you're ready, saying he knows you and he are meant for each other.

Eventually, however, this attention will reveal itself for what it is. Once you're engaged, he'll try to get his way in all wedding decisions. And once you're married, he'll attempt to govern every detail of your life, robbing you of your personhood.

There are at least three ways to test whether the dating behaviors described above stem only from infatuation or also from a desire for control. One is simply to see how he reacts when you don't acquiesce. When you tell him, "I don't want to leave my cell phone on tonight," does he argue or respect your privacy? When you tell him, "If you don't like this outfit, I won't wear it on our dates," does he urge you to stop wearing it altogether or respect your desire to choose your wardrobe? When you tell him, "I'll be spending this Shabbat with friends," does he get upset or respect your right to your own social life? When you tell him, "I'm not ready to decide about marriage," does he pressure you, or respect your need to take your time? As you've noticed, the key to the "correct" response is *respect*—for your independence and your boundaries.

Another sign of control is how he attempts (or doesn't) to resolve conflicts. Does he become angry and shut down emotionally, or can he share his feelings while being sensitive to yours? Must he have his way, or can you work together toward a mutually satisfactory solution?

Perhaps the best barometer of his behavior is your own gut response. Do you avoid arguments as "just not worth it," or can you disagree with him when necessary? Do you always give in so there won't be a fight, or can you express your own desires? When he's mad, does your stomach turn with anxiety, or can you stand up for yourself? Looking not only at him but at *yourself* is a powerful indicator of the health of your relationship.

In the absence of outside information, you can determine if a person is abusive only by spending enough time with him to begin developing emotional intimacy (openness and deep sharing), for this closeness will trigger his true self. Find—or if necessary, create—opportunities to see how he acts when upset, disappointed, angry, or frustrated. Spend time together with family and friends, and ask for their impressions. (Any aversion on his part to such get-togethers is cause for concern.) If someone dislikes something about him, check it out. You may not see it because you don't want to.

After knowing Ruth's fiancé for several months, her mother told her she "didn't feel good" about him. When pressed, all she could specify was his temper. Believing nothing could be wrong, Ruth went ahead with the wedding. Her husband turned out to be highly abusive. Moral of the story: Don't be quick to ignore your mother's intuitions, or those of anyone more objective than you who has your best interests at heart.

As I said in the last chapter, it's important to investigate a person's family life. How did his parents discipline him? Might any traumas lead to abuse? How do his parents relate to each other and their children? While most parents in abusive homes maintain a facade of domestic harmony, you may sense an undercurrent. If your date has rejected the kind of home he came from, he should tell you so, and it must be clear (e.g., from speaking to his therapist) that his childhood wounds have sufficiently healed.

I've also recommended inquiring about his more recent past—activities, friends, and, if relevant, relationships with the opposite sex. (Fear of asking such questions is a bad sign.) If his involvements with women have been insincere or in violation of halacha, does he regret them? Even if he does, one (or more) that was really bad news may indicate a problem. Unhealthy relationships signal an unhealthy personality.

Finally, I've mentioned the importance of input from those who've known him longer and in different circumstances. This information is crucial, as today people often appear on the local dating scene as complete unknowns. What do former employers, teachers, roommates, and others say about him? Reluctance to offer references should immediately push a warning button.

If you observe *several* of the listed traits *repeatedly* in the person you're dating, beware, but don't jump to conclusions. At the same time, don't go into denial, blame yourself, or judge him favorably (an admirable quality but not one meant to be exercised over and over with the same individual). Get a professional opinion. If he has an abusive personality, *get out of the relationship immediately, and ask a rabbi about your obligation to warn others*. If you're not willing to break up, take time out to gain perspective. You may think that because he cares for you more than he's cared for anyone else, or because you'll make him happier than anyone else has, you'll change him. Wrong. Marriage will only bring out the worst in him. Entertaining "rescue" fantasies means you're probably already tolerating treatment you shouldn't. Furthermore, while spiritual guidance must accompany and inform therapy, don't think more Torah study and/or greater religious observance will be the magic cure. Someone scrupulous in observing many religious laws can still behave unethically. Even if he immerses himself in Jewish approaches to character improvement, this is not therapy. *An abusive person will heal only if he admits his dysfunction, wants to change, and gets the help he needs.* And you too will benefit from counseling to understand why you got into this relationship.

Checking Yourself

Now you know how to recognize an abusive person—and *anyone, not matter how emotionally healthy, can become involved with one.* Still, what might increase your chances?

The answer is usually something in your personal history. For example, you may have been overly criticized or emotionally deprived, leaving you low in self-esteem and hungry for love. Think deeply about your childhood. Did your parents accept you as you were, or only when you met their needs and expectations? Look at your patterns today. Do you jump into relationships? Do you cancel plans with a friend whenever a guy shows up? Does your self-worth depend upon another's validation? Do you substitute physical closeness for emotional intimacy? If so, you'll more likely not only attract someone who mistreats you, but lack the self-respect to recognize what's happening. You'll more easily buy his arguments that you cause his misbehavior. And you'll more readily consent to marriage prematurely.

If you don't love yourself enough, you may also fear emotional intimacy (see back in Chapter 2). An abusive relationship is never intimate, so it maintains the emotional distance with which you may be more comfortable.

Another risk factor is having been forced into a parental role at a young age. Did your parents turn to you for nurturance they should have been getting from each other or from friends? Were one or both of them often emotionally or physically absent, leaving you responsible for younger siblings? Abusive individuals are highly immature, crave nurturing desperately, and trigger that familiar feeling of being needed. At the same time, just as in childhood, the energy you devote to caretaking is at the expense of understanding yourself and your own needs.

The strongest factor propelling you into an abusive relationship, however, is what you witnessed growing up. As I've said (in Chapter 3), we all unconsciously gravitate toward what feels familiar, which we consider "normal." If your father abused your mother (or the reverse), you're liable to marry an abuser or abuse your own spouse or children. Sometimes two products of a bad marriage create a good one in which they "rescue" each other from their respective pasts, but rarely. Unless treated, abuse usually passes on to the next generation.

Even if there wasn't actual physical or verbal abuse

in your family, behavior such as frequent yelling can be enough to make abuse seem familiar. Furthermore, wanting your own marriage to be calmer than your parents' may lead to dangerous concessions. A young woman told me regarding the man she later divorced, "When we were dating, I saw his temper, but I was so afraid to re-experience the fighting I saw at home that I always let him have his way." In so doing, she unwittingly empowered him to abuse her.

If you recognize yourself in any of the above descriptions, or if you've already been abused, get competent counseling *now*. If you're addicted to unhealthy relationships, support groups may be even more effective. Don't wait to see if problems arise after marriage. They will—so *do the work first*.

A word of caution to older women, as well as any anxious about their prospects for marriage: Even if you're emotionally solid, desperation can blind you to warning signs (especially if you've been admonished not to be "too picky"). Be careful. You can compromise on a lot and still end up happily married, but not on abusive behavior.

You've learned the warning signs of an abuser—and we must *all* learn them, whether for our own sake or for a friend's. While my own dating career included only nice, normal guys, had I had this information several years ago, I might have been able to prevent a couple of marriages that never should have happened. Take this education with you and pass it on. You'll more likely marry a healthy person with whom you can have a healthy relationship, and help others do the same.

For further reference, see:

- Rabbi Abraham J. Twerski, M.D., *The Shame Borne in Silence: Spouse Abuse in the Jewish Community* (Pittsburgh: Mirov Press, 1996).

  (To order, write P.O.B. 81971, Pittsburgh, PA 15217, or call 1-800-851-8303.)

- Miriam Adahan, *Living with Difficult People (Including Yourself)* (Jerusalem: Feldheim Publishers, 1991), ch. 11.

For advice about a personal situation, call:

- IN THE U.S.:
  Shalom Task Force National Hotline
  In New York: (718) 337-3700
  Outside New York: 1-888-883-2323 (toll-free)

- IN ISRAEL:
  Crisis Center for Religious Women
  Anywhere in the country: (02) 673-0002

- IN OTHER COUNTRIES:
  Contact your local rabbi, synagogue, or Jewish community services.

Part V
Being Informed

Jewish marriage is a spiritual relationship, two people's lifelong commitment to grow together and develop a deep and enduring love. However, it is also a *legal* relationship—and many enter into it without knowing its terms or options. Chapter 8, "Dollars and Sense," discusses the financial side of marriage. Chapter 9, "An Ounce of Prevention," describes a modern solution to giving married women the protection Judaism wants them to have.

Chapter Eight
Dollars and Sense

When I decided to write my first book, I excitedly took the idea to a Jewish publisher. He told me it wouldn't sell, so I'd have to finance it myself and be prepared to incur a loss. More optimistic than he, I was ready to take the chance. Just one thing held me back: the issue of whose money I'd be risking.

Practically speaking, my husband, Avraham, and I treat whatever money we have as "ours." But I was keenly aware that, unless a wife opts to partially support herself, halacha holds the husband responsible for the couple's livelihood, and consequently, he owns any money his wife acquires. Avraham and I had this traditional arrangement, which meant that whatever I earned actually belonged to him. More significantly, "our" savings, with which I would most likely be funding the book, consisted solely of money that Avraham had brought into the marriage and therefore also belonged to him (as my premarital savings, had I had any, would have remained mine). While Avraham was totally behind the project, I got it into my head that I shouldn't gamble with his money.

Shortly afterward, my grandmother (of blessed memory) passed away and left me a monetary gift. I announced to Avraham that I was going ahead with the book since I now had funds of my own. Avraham smiled and said, "Great!" There was something slightly suspicious in his manner, but in my excitement, I ignored it.

A few years later (my hopes for the book's success having been realized), I told Avraham I wanted to put the profits from my first book toward a second one. "It's great to be able to publish my books with my own money," I said happily.

Then he dropped the bomb. "I'm not sure what your grandmother left you, or what you made on it, is really yours," he said.

"What do you mean?" I asked defensively. "My grandmother bequeathed it to me in her will. Of course it's mine."

"I'm not sure about that," was all Avraham would say.

Two years later, the issue came up again in a class taught by a rabbi, and I recounted the story to him.

"I'm sorry to tell you," the rabbi said, "but your husband is most likely correct. It's not enough that your grandmother left the money specifically to you. She also had to stipulate that your husband had no authority over it, which I doubt she did."

So the money was never mine. I was deeply touched that Avraham hadn't let on when I first received it. At the same time, as an educated, religious, married woman, I was upset that I had never known about this law. Had I been in a different kind of marriage, that missing clause might have been very significant.

Making "50-50" a Reality

The basis of Jewish marriage is giving. As such, legalities should play a negligible role.

Nonetheless, Jewish marital law includes financial options that couples should be aware of.

One significant issue is ownership of property and capital. In the Western world today, most women regard themselves as full financial partners in marriage, a status often recognized in civil law. For centuries, Judaism has encouraged couples to view their relationship in this spirit. Indeed, the *tenayim*, the written agreement between two sets of parents stipulating the financial conditions of their children's marriage, states that the couple are to control their assets equally, making all monetary decisions mutually.

While this attitude may be the Jewish ideal, the halacha of actual ownership is different, for the reasons I've explained. This detail may have no practical relevance, unless the couple divorce and the wife requests "her half" of their assets, in which case she'll discover she has no half. Yet even a couple who expect to be happily married for a lifetime may feel uncomfortable with this situation.

To make "50-50" more concrete, you could arrange for a *shtar hilchati* (Jewish legal document) declaring that husband and wife share equally whatever they each bring into the marriage and/or acquire after marrying. This *shtar* can be included as part of a prenuptial agreement, which I'll discuss in the next chapter.

From Parent to Child

Inheritance is another pertinent financial matter. Without the *shtar hilchati* described above, any assets either party inherits become the husband's;

with the *shtar*, they become both his and hers. Many prefer inheritances to remain "in the family," however, belonging only to the actual heir. If either side feels this way, you and your fiancé(e) can sign an agreement in which each party denies any claims to the other's inheritance. (This practice is common in very traditional circles where one or both families are wealthy.) Alternately, if a wife expects to inherit money, she can ask her benefactor to stipulate in the will that "her husband has no authority over it."

My own story ended happily: My husband lovingly let me think the money I inherited was mine, and I published my book. Nevertheless, when it comes to legal matters, ignorance is never a virtue. No matter how good you expect your marriage to be, it pays to know the law.

Chapter Nine
An Ounce of Prevention

On a balmy, starry Chanukah evening, on the lawn of a beautiful moshav just outside Jerusalem, I stood under the *chupa* with my husband-to-be. Avraham recited in Hebrew, "Behold, you are consecrated to me with this ring according to the law of Moses and Israel," and placed the wedding ring on my finger. We were now legally betrothed. Next it was time to read the *ketuba*, the halachic agreement accompanying the marriage.

"I don't care about having a fancy *ketuba*," I had said some weeks earlier. "What's the point in making a work of art out of such a legalistic, unromantic piece of paper?" Avraham had shrugged and said something noncommittal, leaving me to assume he'd probably just use the standard one printed by the Israeli rabbinate.

Now Avraham took out the *ketuba*. But it wasn't what I'd expected. On a beautiful rainbow wash of pastel watercolor, pressed wildflowers framed violet, Hebrew calligraphy—and he had done it all himself. I was stunned and deeply moved. Suddenly I realized how much this "unromantic" piece of paper did mean to me.

The *ketuba* is a central expression of the marriage bond, not only halachically but, in most women's minds, emotionally. Legislated by the rabbis some 2,000 years ago, this document obligates a husband to honor his wife and provide for her needs, including food, clothing, and marital intimacy. Its primary feature, however, specifies the sum he agrees to pay her if he predeceases or divorces her. This pledge is intended to grant her some financial security in either event and to deter him from initiating divorce. In ancient times, investing the amount could produce a steady, long-term income. Today, the figure is usually no more than a few thousand dollars, unless the man chooses to increase it. (Child support remains the husband's responsibility.) The *ketuba* is considered so important that a couple may not live together as husband and wife without it.

Unfortunately, while the *ketuba* retains its emotional significance and occupies a prominent place on many living room walls, relying on it to protect women in the event of divorce has become a major problem.

Ideal and Reality

Sarah and Michael, an engaged couple in their mid-20s, sat down to plan their wedding. The band, hall, caterer, and invitation list were soon agreed upon. The next topic was the *ketuba*—who would design it, and what sum would be recorded therein. As Michael came from a wealthy family, Sarah expected him to add significantly to the minimum amount.

"Let's use the number 18," Michael proposed romantically, referring to the numerical value of the word *chai*, life. "I'll have the *ketuba* written for $18,000."

Sarah was taken aback. "What's the matter?" Michael asked. "You don't like 18?"

"I do... but..."

"But what?"

With what she hoped was a cute grin, Sarah said, "How about adding another zero?"

Michael didn't know what to respond. Sensing the need for guidance, the two approached Rabbi Friedman, a respected community leader and *posek* known for his straight talk.

"Well, there's good news and bad news," he informed them. "The good news is you needn't worry whether to write the *ketuba* for $18,000 or $180,000, because it really doesn't matter. Most men have life insurance policies whose value far exceeds the *ketuba*. And when couples divorce, they almost always divide their assets according to considerations such as who'll have custody of the children and each party's financial needs. So you can move on to the fun stuff, like who's going to do the artwork and calligraphy."

"Okay," Sarah said uneasily. "What's the bad news?"

"The bad news," Rabbi Friedman continued soberly, "is that Jews today live under the jurisdiction of secular governments, so no matter how much money the wife is entitled to, a *beit din* [rabbinical court] can't ensure that she gets it."

The couple were shocked—especially Sarah. How come she never knew this?

"If there's a divorce," the rabbi went on, "a decent man may give his wife a fair settlement, particularly if he really wants out. But if his wife feels more strongly about leaving the marriage than he does, there can be big problems. Jewish divorce requires mutual consent. Therefore, the husband can hold out for anything he wants in exchange for his agreement."

"But why would a man behave like that?" Michael wondered aloud.

"Michael," Rabbi Friedman explained, "divorce is a time of tremendous ill will, and anger can overcome decency. Each party blames the other, and he who walks away with most of the couple's assets and custody of the kids can feel vindicated. He can proclaim: 'See, if I was awarded all this, the divorce can't be my fault.' "

The young man shook his head. "I can't picture someone doing that."

"I'm glad, but unfortunately it does happen—and while a woman can treat her husband the same way, it's far less common. Furthermore, if the wife defies the *beit din*'s ruling and refuses to accept a divorce, her husband can attempt to obtain what's called a *heter meah rabbanim*, 'permission of 100 rabbis.' While granted only in certain cases, it allows him to override the 1,000-year-old ban on having more than one wife—which Biblical law permitted—and marry another woman. A woman whose husband denies her a divorce has no such option."

"Can't the rabbis do anything to help her?" Sarah wanted to know.

"They can try," Rabbi Friedman replied. "They can post notices telling people to bar her husband from every synagogue, boycott his business, and otherwise ostracize him—in other words, they can make his life so difficult that he may give in. In Israel, the government can strip him of many rights and privileges and even jail him. In Chassidic communities, the rebbe may send a bunch of his followers to 'persuade him non-verbally' to give the divorce. Other communities have employed their own creative solutions. But if nothing works, the wife is stuck. And aside from her suffering, it's a terrible *chillul Hashem* [desecration of God's name], since it appears as if Judaism doesn't care about women."

There was a long silence. Sarah glanced over at Michael, awaiting his response.

"Rabbi Friedman," Michael finally said, "neither Sarah nor I have any doubt that our marriage is going to last. Even if we're wrong, God forbid, I can't imagine treating my wife unfairly. But if the *ketuba* no longer protects women, I don't think we want to bury our heads in the sand."

Inwardly relieved, Sarah added, "I doubt my parents will want us to either. While they think the world of Michael and feel as good about our relationship as we do, they'd be pretty upset knowing that their daughter is marrying without any protection."

Rabbi Friedman nodded. "You've each raised important points, and I agree with them. But there's an issue here that's larger than you or your parents. That's concern for *klal Yisrael* [the entire Jewish people]. Most religious Jewish women will never be divorced. But a minority will—and for their sake, it's important that the wedding ceremony include a halachic agreement that can protect them."

Restoring Protection

If you're bothered by the state of Jewish divorce today, you can demonstrate responsibility for *klal Yisrael* by signing a halachic prenuptial agreement.

Some people associate prenuptial agreements with those used in civil marriages to ensure that, in the likely event of divorce, both parties "gets theirs." A Jewish prenuptial agreement, however, simply restores to women the basic protection the *ketuba* once provided by using civil courts to enforce its terms. A prenuptial agreement thus preserves the spirit and intent of Jewish law and is appropriate in even the most traditional religious circles. Prominent rabbinical authorities who endorse prenuptial agreements include Rabbi Zalman Nechemyah Goldberg of Jerusalem's highest rabbinical court, and Dayan Chanoch Ehrentreu of the London *beit din*, whose formulation is approved by Rabbi Yosef Shalom Elyashiv of Jerusalem and is used throughout the United Kingdom.

In the most common prenuptial agreement, both parties agree that if either wants to dissolve the marriage, the case will be decided by a specific *beit din*, and each will pay spousal support for every day he or she withholds or rejects the bill of divorce the court has ordered. The document can also divide the couple's assets 50-50, by including the *shtar hilchati* described in the last chapter. A prenuptial agreement thus helps end a marriage with dignity, not mistreatment. An authority in Jerusalem's rabbinical court directorate estimates that halachically binding prenuptial agreements could eliminate 90% of the problem of husbands refusing to grant a divorce or wives refusing to accept one.

Despite the benefits of a prenuptial agreement, a couple wanting one may encounter well-meaning opposition. When intellectual, the concern is usually based on the content of the agreement. A halachic divorce must be voluntary. The greater the financial consequences imposed on the uncooperative partner, the greater the risk of coercing a divorce. On the other hand, the smaller the consequences, the less effectual the prenuptial mechanism will be. Fortunately, versions exist that have met with rabbinical approval *and* prevented unethical behavior in divorce proceedings. (Indeed, some rabbis are so convinced of the agreement's benefits that they won't officiate at weddings without one.)

Most objections to prenuptial agreements, however, are emotional. One young woman I know was asked, "Why start your marriage with one foot out the door?" Yet by merely reinstating safeguards like those provided by the *ketuba*, a Jewish prenuptial agreement presumes no less trust between bride and groom or optimism about the marriage's success. The *ketuba* itself is actually a 2,000-year-old prenuptial agreement—and like its forebear, the modern variety indicates the seriousness of a couple's commitment and belief in their marriage. As one advocate puts it, "The public has to be educated that signing a prenuptial agreement is not a declaration of war but an act of love."

Other couples may be told, "In our community, it's not done." Discomfort with something unfamiliar is understandable. However, "it's not done" is a poor reason to neglect something that perhaps *should* be done.

A particularly male reason for eschewing a prenuptial agreement may be self-interest. While the agree-

ment protects both parties in a marriage, it is generally employed for the woman's sake. A man might
therefore ask, "Why would a guy want to sign this?" I
would in turn ask him, "Why would a guy want to
give his wife a *ketuba*?" The answer to both questions
is simple: because he understands that Judaism wants
women to be protected in marriage. Indeed, if a man
appreciates the purpose of a prenuptial agreement
and still refuses to sign one, he is in effect saying, "If
we get divorced, I want to be able to hurt you."

Most common, however, is the "icky" reaction:
"Why would you want such an icky, unromantic document to be part of your wedding?" I always find this
concern humorous, since the *ketuba* itself, viewed as a
beautiful statement of marital commitment, primarily
declares how much the husband owes his wife if he
divorces her. You can't get more "icky" and unromantic than that. We're just accustomed to the *ketuba*, and
not to prenuptial agreements. Perhaps the solution is
for prenuptial agreements to become as universal as
the *ketuba*, which many rabbis feel they are destined to
be.

When you were young and had to be vaccinated,
you undoubtedly protested, "I don't need to! I
won't get sick!" If the disease in question was generally avoided by maintaining hygiene, you were probably correct. But because the Department of Health
can't single out unhygienic people for vaccinations—
and because, no matter how clean you are, disease can
strike—everyone must be immunized. It's a matter of
public health.

Prenuptial agreements are similar—and it was

with this concern for the Jewish people that my friend Marina presented the idea to her husband-to-be. "I know neither of us will ever need it," she told him, "but for the sake of those who will, I'd like it to become standard practice for everyone in *klal Yisrael*. So I want us to help make that happen." And he agreed.

You too can make a prenuptial agreement part of your wedding, along with a public statement explaining why. In the opinion of an increasing number of rabbis and young couples, it's one way of saying, "I care."

A Final Word

Being a Jewish single means walking a fine line. You should always be preparing and longing for marriage; at the same time, you must live fully now. The trick is to do things that provide pleasure and satisfaction and simultaneously increase your chances of finding your soulmate.

First and foremost, this strategy means growing spiritually. Judaism teaches that the world stands on three things: Torah study, prayer, and acts of kindness. So does your spiritual well-being. Even if you're an up-and-coming Torah scholar, you need to do *chesed*; even if you're always helping others, you need to learn; and everyone needs to speak to God, honestly and often. All will feed your mind, heart, and soul, increase your self-worth, and make you an even more promising partner for someone special.

Working and supporting yourself can also build the self-esteem necessary to a healthy relationship. But choose a career carefully. If you're serious about getting married, no amount of money or job satisfaction is worth lowering your chances. A young attorney told me that when she realized litigation was making her nasty, she switched to tax law, a far less exciting field but one where she could preserve the character traits she wanted to bring to her future marriage. That's a smart lawyer.

No matter how much you're earning, if you want experience in living with another person, consider a roommate. Learning to share space, divide responsibilities, and get along with someone different from you is among the best preparation for married life.

Beyond building character, develop any and all talents and abilities that don't conflict with finding your soulmate. Learn about new things. Broaden your horizons. You'll be more interesting and alive, and more people will want to spend time with you. You'll also be more attractive. Someone once asked a well-known rebbetzin for her favorite beauty tip. She replied, "Education. It puts light in your eyes." So too for a myriad of other activities. Do what lights you up.

Yet don't ignore your physical well-being. If you're an armchair slug and junk food addict, maybe it's time to get moving and start eating right. Becoming healthier and more fit may be challenging, but you'll love the results.

Of all the pursuits I've mentioned, *chesed* should top your list. *Give to others.* Use your talents and abilities to enrich not only your own life but theirs. You'll see how truly blessed you are, and the genuine happiness that results from devoting yourself to a worthy project, whether a nationwide cause or a next-door neighbor's needs. And at the same time, you'll develop the quality most meaningful to a lifelong, loving relationship.

So while continuing to work toward marriage, don't put your life on hold. There's too much to do in this world. Go out and give. You'll be richer for it— and your growth will bring you closer to that special day you're waiting for.

About the Author

Gila Manolson (née Marilyn Fisch) grew up in the northeastern United States and graduated magna cum laude from Yale University with a degree in music. She later studied at Neve Yerushalayim College for Women. For five years, she was resident supervisor of the women's branch of Heritage House, a Jewish youth hostel in Jerusalem's Old City. She has taught in numerous programs and is a popular lecturer in Israel and abroad. She is also the author of *The Magic Touch: A Jewish Approach to Relationships* and *Outside/Inside: A Fresh Look at Tzniut*. She and her husband live in Jerusalem with their seven children.